From the Italian Girl To Cabaret

Musical Humour, Parody and Burlesque

by

D1578610

George Colerick, BA BSc (Econ)

Published by

JUVENTUS

LONDON

JUVENTUS Publications include:
New Chekhovs (1998)
Romanticism and Melody (1995)

First published in 1998 by JUVENTUS, 81 Lumley Courtyard,
Holbein Place, London SW1W 8LU

British Library Cataloguing-in-Publication Data

A catalogue record for this book
is available from the British Library

ISBN 0 952496437

Cover by Mark Hedge
Typeset by York House Typographic
Printed and bound by J. W. Arrowsmith Ltd, Bristol

Contents

Y0045362

Foreword

Janáček's *Mr Broucek*, as we performers discover, is a very problematic work, and I have even tended to regard the two *Excursions* separately; but remarkably, Mr Colerick has articulated a link between them, so giving a fresh perspective about this opera by the composer who was once my teacher.

The author does not go for the easy options, and his humorous selections have purposes well beyond the obvious. It was adventurous to write about a most unusual work by Gustav Holst, a man whose idiosyncratic approach to composing I have specially admired. George Colerick has approached masterpieces by Rossini and Strauss with sharp historical insight, and the broad picture of Suppé should raise curiosity about his neglected vocal music.

Without becoming too technical, the author shows how certain composers of intrinsically funny music achieve their effects. He also gives persuasive reasons for what we too rarely enjoy today, the staging of quality musicals which create laughter.

Through his style and sense of humour, I have come to a close musical understanding of the writer, and believe this is an even better book than his previous one. It is informative and diverting for layman and musician alike. (Vilem Tausky, C.B.E.)

Amusing and authoritative. This book is a treasury of information, much of which has been a revelation to me. (Ned Sherrin)

List of Illustrations

Preface
(especially for young readers)

A Canadian publisher once suggested I should write a joke book on music, but I was not tempted. There was a more engaging project to approach, partly because musical humour is a vast, sprawling topic which has been too rarely dealt with in a specialised manner. Recent books on burlesques – what we now call 'send-ups' – are difficult to find even in the public libraries.

Elements of burlesque and parody are very prominent on television and elsewhere, occasionally with imaginative use of music. Certain film directors with a fine musical sensibility, such as Stanley Kubrick and Woody Allen, select attractive material which has strongly humorous or ironic effects. An incongruous background can add greatly to the fun; a *Dracula* spoof by Barry Humphries, one of the best filmed, had mock-Gothic scenes to *Duke Bluebeard's Castle* by Bartok. Then a clergyman had a fist-fight with his twin brother to Bach's renowned Toccata and Fugue. In the finale, a preposterous 'lady' was joined by the real Australian Prime Minister.

A *Monty Python* sketch featured a most seductive housewife luring a milkman into an upstairs room where he found himself with some dozen other imprisoned milkmen. A *Spitting Image* Prime Minister calmly balanced peas on a fork whilst the radio blasted out a fearsome din. Both scenes were extremely funny even if one was only affected by the music subliminally. It would be interesting to know what proportion of listeners recognised what was being played and how far that added to their enjoyment. The 'seduction' was carried out to a sensual passage from *Tristan and Isolde*; the Prime Minister eventually turned off the noise – it was the 'Day of Judgment' (*Dies irae*) from Verdi's *Requiem*.

I would hesitate to tell an enquiring stranger the central theme of this book, because that might cause confusion – music written in our times is scarcely associated with sophisticated humour. That combination, once broadly taken for granted, is now elevated to a cult, so these chapters may help to widen the circle of those who enjoy it, through recordings, on the stage or T.V.

We as consumers are constantly being demoralised and desensitised by the media; nearly half of us, statistically at least, are said to look forward to negative news bulletins about death, destruction, calamity and conflict, from whichever part of the world it may be scavenged. Media 'entertainment' largely consists of soap operas which peddle human suffering and rage, even under the pretence of realism: lyrics of popular songs express frustration and self-pity, and films are loaded with verbal and physical violence. Ironically, many people's introduction to great melodies is now coming through television ads.

Our ancestors, who might have worked hard for 50 hours a week without being able to afford a holiday, were offered glorious music as an escape, even if only on a barrel-organ, friendly and enjoyable even for its misplaced rhythms. Music halls were set on cheering people up, with misfortunes always turned into jokes; even creepy Victorian melodramas had happy endings, and early Hollywood used similar formulae.

At what age should one start listening to good music? I had none at home or school (preferring football to my piano lessons), so was quite old when setting-out alone and resolute on this, until then by far the greatest adventure of my life – nearly 17, and in my earliest enthusiasms, Tchaikovsky, Beethoven and Brahms, I was certainly not looking for humour. Yet within months, I had an experience which was to encourage my taste for the absurd.

Music had no part in the event, attending a performance of a classic burlesque, Richard Sheridan's *Critic*; I was surprised at finding it excessively funny, considering we were then enjoying it, but without much laughter, in the sixth form. Even so, it was some years before I began to take that and related styles of entertainment seriously, eventually becoming addicted to Offenbach and others.

At 16, I knew that Mozart had written some very amusing operas, and two of my friends had cycled over 100 miles to see one of them; this feat was regarded by the rest of our school with tolerant bemusement, and the two of them were simply branded as 'mad'. I realised they shared something valuable which I must discover.

Wit is a quality to be found in all the greatest composers, but to write original music which is intrinsically funny is far more difficult than preparing solemn but uninspired melodies, which most of us could write after one month of studying theory.

From childhood there was no shortage of funny music I liked, and the best may now be listed among popular classics: some humorous jazz, the self-mockery of 'Blues in the Night', the music and lyrics of the Gershwins. The exuberance and fun of central European songs were denied us in the repertoire of 'popular' music, but something of those spirits was to be conveyed, thanks to America's immigrant Jewish composers.

Adding to tapings of musical farces has been a rare pleasure over years. Serious, passionate music is best heard and assimilated when one is young and learning the tragedy of life; growing older, it is better to laugh as much as possible.

I can testify to this through a curious sequence of events. As an undergraduate, I came out of a performance of Strauss' *Salome* in a trance, and with the pubs all closing at ten, nowhere to go to celebrate an overwhelming experience with two friends. Unimaginable that some forty years later I'd be writing a chapter about a filmed send-up of this *Salome*.

The conductor that night was Vilem Tausky, who nearly monopolised BBC Radio on one occasion by performing *Salome* live (the famed Salvador Dali production) whilst his pre-recording for the *Al Read Show* went out on the BBC Light Programme. Some years ago, he took special pleasure conducting and playing a small role in a filmed burlesque, Mozart's hilarious *Impresario*. Also as a composer, he has had a foot in both light and serious camps; when a young man, three of his operettas were successfully produced in his native Moravia. Perhaps they would have been good material for a chapter in this book if the Nazis had not destroyed them.

I have enjoyed evenings of light music as far as Budapest, Warsaw, Moscow and Kiev, but have related as far as possible to works which our readers may have a chance to see or obtain on recordings. Only because I have already written about their style at some length, the witty Prokofiev and Chabrier are omitted, also Jules Massenet whose opera, *Griselidis* (1901), sketches the 'concern' of the Devil for the wife of an absent crusader.

One form of 'parody' will not be dealt with in these chapters – commercial plagiarism. In my book on melody, I cited Massenet's most passionate music as having 'inspired' much popular French music in the following decades. In connection with chapter 23, I'd just add that his opera, *Herodiade*, a much romanticised version of the Salome story, has a theme related to John the Baptist. It has reappeared in a very popular British musical, and in a religious context.

There are invisible cultural threads between the finest works of European burlesque. Whatever material one chooses, certain characters, songs and concepts are likely to reappear: Jupiter and other Roman gods, the Trojan war, Turkish pashas, foolish commanders, 'God save the Queen', cuckoldry, 'The Carnival of Venice'. The two who keep popping up right to the final pages of this book are Mephisto and the diabolical Robert – of whom more later.

My selection of elaborated themes from comedy and farce includes some dozen womanizers and/or fools who get their come-uppance. Lechery always lurks, but is contained and the women are decidedly in command. If you prefer to read of pure love, idealistic men and adoring females, this book is not for you.

G.A.C.

Acknowledgements

I would like very much to thank the following: Ursula Vaughan Williams for expanding on her husband's approach to Falstaff and related themes; Vilem Tausky and Ned Sherrin for their sympathetic interest, and lending me valuable data; Geoffrey Brawn, Director of the Players Theatre, London, for the loan of material, including lyrics by Maurice Browning; Dr Lucile Desblache for helping me with Hervé's naughty French stories; and the Metropol Theater, Berlin, for a fine choice of photographic material.

1   *The Parisian Music Theatre After 1850*

Paris – The Second Empire (1852–70) – Modernisation and Material Advancement!

The régime of Emperor Louis Napoleon III spent wisely on replanning the city and launching the prestigious international exhibitions of 1855 and 1867. Paris could claim to be the cultural and entertainment centre for Europe's leaders and social elites. Its accepted image in that period and the years after is seen in the vitality and colour of the great contemporaneous paintings, highlighting the Boulevards, pleasure gardens, theatre interiors and dancing girls.

In the supposed interests of culture, a handful of theatres had for half a century monopolistic privileges which remained until the year 1858 and restricted the staged activities of potential competitors. French classical tragedy, modern romantic drama and exemplary grand opera enjoyed prestige throughout Europe.

Grand opera had developed since the days of the Revolution when massive stage displays had served political ends, inciting powerful feelings among the citizens. Later, the emphasis was upon bourgeois values and spiritual struggles, the drama of good and evil. The Paris Opera building of Charles Garnier's 1867 design symbolised the full splendour of Europe's artistic tradition, and for the French, grand opera was the finest form of musical expression. The accepted model was very lengthy, four to five acts, sung entirely in French without dialogue, but with spectacular ballet integrated into the action.

There was in addition an important Italian language opera house. In the '60s, the Lyrique, a commercial theatre which was less hide-bound, produced distinguished operas and attracted younger composers such as Charles Gounod.

Opera-comique was a style which had attracted very many composers in the early 19th century, and had its own famous house with the same descriptive name. Such works were not necessarily lighter in theme and treatment, and the term opera-comique had no obvious associations with humour. They had the advantage of spoken dialogue and by convention avoided tragic endings.

This 'high' culture was paralleled by a 'Boulevard' culture, given coherence by the increasing number of broadsheets; it attracted writers, artists, the 'golden youth', rich foreigners, Bohemians, adventurers and 'dandies' living off their investments. There were men and women of the stage to work in commercial entertainment, which could satisfy a growing range of tastes medium- and low-brow. Prominent were the vaudevilles – slight plays with songs to familiar melodies enlivened by new lyrics – harlequinades and pantomimes.

The city population doubled during the two Imperial decades to two million, and from the 1870s about one quarter was attending a theatre at least once a week, enough to fill every night a hundred of the larger ones. Splendid, recently-built railway stations greeted visitors from all parts of Europe, a new style of tourism with the affluent finding the stage a major attraction.

Premières at leading opera houses drew the elite in the creative arts, political and business leaders, socialites and foreign dignitaries. Europe's capital cities were building prestigious opera houses in similar style to those of Paris and the great Italian cities. The realisation of spectacular productions influenced later entertainments, notably in the European film industries and Hollywood in its earlier years, even without accompanying music scores.

During the 19th century, grand opera by combining all the creative arts achieved immense aesthetic and social importance, and as a result became very controversial, quite apart from financial considerations. The criteria had been heightened by the intensely dramatic works of Jakob Meyerbeer, which called for the finest operatic voices and resources, and the largest theatres, from the appearance of his *Robert le Diable* in 1829, through to *L'Africaine (1865)*.

2 Paris – London: The Versatile Monsieur Hervé

The success of Florimond Hervé in London of the 1870s and '80s is an interesting parallel to the appeal for later generations of the Marx Brothers and *Monty Python*. His earlier achievements in France developed from an exceptional talent in light theatre music often written in great haste for popular shows.

Composing for the Church enabled him to support a mother who had performed menial work for years. Aged 14, he became church organist at Bicêtre and was soon writing stage works to be performed by inmates at a nearby asylum, a remarkable experiment in psycho-therapy, and one which came to interest the medical world. There were many incidents in his life that reveal him as a benign spirit.

Composing witty music is a rare gift, and he was keen to make it his priority, whereas Arthur Sullivan, in a comparable situation, desired above all the prestige of being regarded as a 'serious' composer.

Hervé's flair for musical burlesque first came to public attention after a short, rounded actor asked the tall, slim 23-year old Hervé for an entertainment in which both of them could act and sing; his choice was an adaptation of *Don Quixote and Sancho Panza* (1848). Its combination of outright farce, a 'buffoonery', with specially composed music made it an innovation, what was soon to be known as opera *bouffe*.[1]

He raised the stakes by collaborating with other writers, and burlesques of existing theatrical styles were noted at court circles in 1853. After a private showing for the Emperor, Hervé declined an official post, fearing that it would restrict his artistic freedom. Instead he requested and obtained permission for a small theatre to be a workshop for developing his style of entertainment, to become well known as the Folies-Nouvelles.

He possessed musicianship, an instinct for the theatre and

total dedication. With musicals restricted under his licence to two actor-singers, he could indulge his fancy for playing several parts, male or female, with quick changes, so he could write more elaborate plots. Why not set-up singing corpses, dumb singers and off-stage noises, forcing the censor to laugh at the infringements? With choruses illegal and too costly, the dancers, crowds, and anything suggesting space could be painted on set. Experiments were made with moving scenery, trapdoors, real and pantomime animals and cardboard props. Hervé was on the way to a big reputation as master of stage illusion.

He encouraged other young talents, producing their smaller stage works, and in this way Leo Delibes had some success in operettas, though now better known as composer of ballets, and two exquisite 'popular' arias from the opera *Lakmé*.

After two years and several minor successes, he quit the small theatre, seeking wider experience, and began to enjoy working at the Eldorado, a leading music hall. When legal limitations on staged music ended, versatile artistes were available in numbers. In general, the men were comedians with sufficiently strong voices and a sense of rhythm; the women were trained singers able to switch at once from opera to farce and lively dancing.

Sophisticated parody should be a compliment to great art. Hector Berlioz was not favoured by Paris' operatic establishment, and in 1863, his frustration deepened with an inadequate production of what is now considered a masterpiece, *The Trojans*. He would have felt no pleasure at inspiring a 'sequel'; claiming to be a quick worker, Hervé had within weeks prepared his own *Trojans at Champagne*.

His first large musical centred on the legend of King Arthur. Grand spectaculars were to be staged, seen at their best in *The Turks*[2] (1869), a parody of a classic 17th century tragedy by Racine. No literary skills are needed to enjoy harem guards lamenting their eunuch status, a barcarolle for bathing odalisques, and a chorus of mutes. To meet the growing fashion in European capitals for things 'Asian', Hervé weighed in with a song for Georgian women.

L'Oeil crevé (One in the Eye), 1867–8, was the first work to acquire an international reputation, a surreal treatment of archery 'inspired' by Weber's *Freischütz*, and with anachronisms a major source of laughter. The music was widely admired and the *Figaro* critic even praised its harmonic subtleties.

Historical characters were to be cut down to size, and then some, though Chilperic, a 6th century Frankish king, starts impressively on a real horse, then boasts of his female conquests in the *Butterfly* song which became a favourite. He takes a peasant girl as mistress, allowing her fiancé to enjoy himself with the ladies of the court; deserted by the King in the second act, she plots his downfall. By then murder is in everyone's head, which must be a relief after so much philandering. Hervé played the title role, quickly gaining box-office triumphs and *Chilperic* was to be popular for decades. Toulouse Lautrec attended performances often during the '90s and painted Marcelle Lender dancing a bolero before the royal assemblage[3].

This work and *Petit Faust*, an outrageous parody of Gounod's *Faust*, were further enhanced by the charismatic Blanche d'Antigny, a youthful, brilliant self-publicist, playing alongside Hervé. *Le beau monde* attended each new production, men such as Flaubert and Renoir being enthusiasts. Hervé's 'epics' continued to appear through the '70s, and fittingly, a dramatisation of Rabelais' *Panurge* (1879) included songs based upon some of that 16th century writer's unbridled texts. It was Hervé's farewell to spectaculars; after that, he completed only the 'chamber works', vaudeville-operettas, which were in fashion, *Mam'zelle Nitouche* and *Lili* the best known.

Edward, Prince of Wales, was an enthusiast of female stars and light musicals, even proposing humorous stage additions, and suggested Hervé should perform in London.

The disruption of Parisian life in the war of 1870–71 made him take up the idea and learn English. In no time, he was playing title roles in *Chilperic* and *Petit Faust* at London's Lyceum theatre, his accent being an extra cause for humour. This marked the start of his association with England spanning two decades, bringing early stage successes at Drury Lane and the Gaiety.

The critics accepted that *Chilperic* was London's landmark in theatrical presentation, and (the *Sportsman*) ... *an opera bouffe* at once remarkably funny and grandly spectacular. It contained *vocal and instrumental novelties to entrance the ear* (*Sporting and Dramatic News*), not least the artiste who could turn himself into a moaning bassoon. The *Daily Telegraph* said it *teemed with things beautiful and amusing*, but that the music was a weak dilution of Offenbach, Gounod and Meyerbeer. One indignant critic wrote of *funereal gags and stale wheezes against the present government*.

London would experience an invasion of French musicals in the '70s and Mr H.B. Farnie undertook most translations for London theatres; granted that he was trying to conform to public taste, the following lyrics do no justice to the original:

> *I have a mistress soft and kind;*
> *If ever I am dull or queer,*
> *Believe or not, she need but smile*
> *And soon her charms will cheer* . . . .
> *My mistress is wine, rosy wine.*

Hervé had written the words of *Chilperic*, here referring to physical intimacy, the singer's mistress being likened to a bottle which he drinks in large gulps:

> *J'adore ma brune maîtresse dont le gai babil m'étourdi,*
> *Voluptueusement je presse sa taille et goûte son esprit,*
> *Cette maîtresse sanspareille et qui ne me trompe jamais,*
> *C'est ma délicieuse bouteille que toujours je vide à longs traits.*

The memoires of Emily Soldine, who often sang leads for Hervé, are witness to his exceptional stage personality, especially in this role:

> 'Such gaiety, grace, and perfection of style, expressive hands . . . . . . not much voice but what wonders he did with it . . . . . . the charming way he carried off Fredegonde and promised to love her for ever in the first act, and did not love her at all in the second but danced the cancan and chaffed and aggravated her till she had hysterics and threw her shoe at him . . . . . . No wonder the women went down in regiments before this foreign fascinator.'

His *Aladdin II*, specially written for London, was a 26-number adult musical which sought to match visually the fantasies of childhood, with a magic toyshop, underwater grotto and diving bell. These stagings were all the more impressive nearly 20 years before electricity reached most theatres.

Mam'zelle Nitouche (1883) is a musical within a musical, partly autobiographical, opening with a confidential address to the audience:

'So I'm back – hope no-one sees me this time of the morning. To think that I'm Celestin, church organist as well as teaching girls at the Convent of the Swallows, but I just have to jump over that wall every evening ...... let's face it, quite bizarre. You ask why a respectable, clean-living young man should spend half his nights away from this holy residence. You see, I've written an operetta, *Babet et Cadet*. One month ago, I showed my manuscript to a leading council official who is keen to run his own shows. Within days, I had chosen the stage-name Floridor, and was billed as the composer to put our community on the map.'

Sacred and profane in uneasy tandem. When the keenest pupil, Denise, plays truant, it is because she is learning to understudy the lead role in *Babet*, and gives herself the stage-name, *Mam'zelle Nitouche* (Miss Hands-off). The community theatre is fun, much less innocently off-stage, and during the school's music lessons, the girls take any opportunity of introducing Celestin's comic songs into their prayers. Even in an age when good melodies grew on trees, Hervé's music had an unusually spicy appeal.

A farcical episode adds a military flavour and drum rolls to the score when Nitouche dresses as a soldier in order to enter the barracks. One London critic complained that an unescorted girl spending the night with soldiers was not suitable for staging; but the English translation was saving him further embarassment. The original lyrics were risqué, telling how along the rue de la Fayette, she bumped into a young soldier and his musical instrument.

In French, praying to the mythical sainte Nitouche is a metaphor for acting the innocent, which Denise does in child-like song; how could a pure convent girl have become pregnant? Hervé had lived for years like Celestin-Floridor and married his pupil, but probably not because he had to.

Mam'zelle Nitouche is a modest little comedy compared with the works on which Hervé's fame was created, but it has been filmed twice and if it is performed more than the others today, that is because of its charm, well-constructed libretto and ease of production.

In 1884, Hervé was appointed as musical director of London's new prestige theatre, the 3,000 seater Empire, and *Chilperic* was the predictable choice for the opening. Among the ballets Hervé composed for its stage, there was one dedicated to English and Scottish sports. We are left to imagine what use he made of an England-Australia test match, hunting in Leicestershire or (according to a programme) a *pas de deux* by the 'Ladies of the Future' at the Henley regatta.

He had long since been associated with London's big musical events. For its 1873 Promenade season, he was appointed conductor at an exceptional salary, and in one week, attendance reached 20,000 with over one quarter on the evening of Hervé's music. There was temporary fame for his serious symphonic composition. *The Battle of Ashanti*, performed at Covent Garden, and at a time when Beethoven symphonies were rarely heard, he performed them in London and Paris.

Despite his dynamism, Hervé was far from difficult as a collaborator, and London impresario John Hollingshead wrote of him as a 'quiet French gentleman'. His rapport with England extended to marrying a Nottingham girl, but not before making one more theatrical gesture: a public declaration of celibacy, his wife having 'disappeared' some 20 years previously. He took British nationality, and to facilitate journeys to Paris, lived in Folkestone where his children were schooled. By the '90s he had removed them to Paris, where, sensitive behind the clown's mask, he died in 1892 as a result of an asthma attack brought on by severe criticism of his last work, *Bacchanal.*

His intended epitaph was: *J'ai fait rire* – I made people laugh.

■ ■ ■

Hervé's stage works offered untamed humour, dazzling productions with inventive gimmicks and exciting dance troupes. But by the '80s, the trend was away from licentious musicals towards more decorous, sentimental works. After his vogue had passed, an authoritative French encyclopaedia of opera published in 1905 reflected the reaction against his work, condemning its 'deliberate' vulgarity, especially of language. Even at that date, official Paris society would respond with disgust at any attempted display of nudity, though what was going on in low dives was another matter; yet four decades earlier, Hervé's productions, as Soldine wrote approvingly, had been displaying the beauty and agility of chorus girls' bodies. She did not mention that in the Paris *Chilperic*, throwing one's shoe at the King would have been very tame; his mistress threw in all her clothes.

'Vulgarities' deplored by many critics were later to be eliminated, but looking back on a century of the genre (1865–1965), *L'Histoire de l'operette en France* concluded that the 'more refined' styles (apparent in the 20th century and early European and Hollywood films) were not a progression:

> *dénouements with docile lovers proposing to insipid valse-duets which delight no-one.*

L'Histoire sees Hervé as one of the two most exciting composers of French opera *bouffe*. It points to his integrity and the help he gave other talents. He was a Bohemian enjoying exceptional artistic freedom, knowing fulfilment among the theatres of the Boulevards, a creator of healthy laughter and euphoria, his music variable in quality but always 'honest'.

Hervé had many critics. He could be very wasteful of his melodic gifts, and was often too rushed to write sophisticated harmonies, whilst his frequent use of very basic rhythms might suggest a 'popular' rather than an 'art' composer. Yet *L'Histoire* calls him a master of wit, rhythm and orchestration. Only the anarchic nature of many scripts prevents authentic performances today, but among the two-hundred or so music scores, it rates highest *The Turks, Panurge*, and a bizarre historical, *The Throne of Scotland*, along with those which were also very successful in English translation, *L'Oeil crevé, Chilperic* and *Petit Faust*.

These three should be revived, according to a most authoritative book for our times, Richard Traubner's comprehensive *Operetta* (revised 1989). He points out that Hervé is still performed in Eastern Europe, and describes *Petit Faust* as 'a wonderful score'.

3 *Faust and a Burlesque*

The obscure German legend of Faust had been revived by Christopher Marlowe and Goethe, and by the 19th century it had entered into Christian consciousness as a morality, setting worldly temptations against eternal salvation. To the young Romantics, it was a specially attractive theme, the individual defying social mores, and destroying himself in abandonment to his feelings.

Liszt, Berlioz, Boito, Busoni and Gounod were inspired to compose important works. Mephistopheles, or Mephisto as he became affectionately known, was seen in part a comic character, a subject for burlesque. He might be in children's books, almost a homely figure in quaint red costume, or quite fearsome with red features indicating that he was roasting in hell.

This image accorded with the times. In Catholic France, as a participant in a morality, he had a 'religious' function so that his presentation on any stage was a sensitive issue. He should be seen, at best, as one to be laughed at, hence the ridiculous costume. Then to emphasise his lack of humanity, two horns and a tail were added.

1859 was the year Charles Gounod launched his *Faust*, to a text by Jules Barbier and Michel Carré whose skills also served Meyerbeer, Thomas and Offenbach. It was to become for decades the most popular opera in the world, through its melodic inspiration, colourful and dramatic scenes and an attractive musical sketching of Mephisto. As he uses magic to assist Faust in the gratification of the senses, his tricks, disguises and mocking serenade give him a genial aspect. This makes him even more unsuited to combat with God, so the opera's central theme seems lightweight.

Gounod's version had centred on the Marguerite episode, Goethe's first important addition to the original legend, used as a love story unexceptional in an opera of modest proportions with three principal singers, and it suited the requirements of the Opera Comique. He had no cause to fear competition from the idiosyncratic *Damnation of Faust* written and composed as early as 1845 by Berlioz who was totally out of favour with Paris' opera establishment. This likewise portrayed Marguerite as the trusting victim of evil forces, seduced and driven to despair, but judged blameless.

Berlioz' was a work of genius, not even intended as an opera, but a dramatic cantata, with action subordinated to atmosphere, motivation and character. The magical aspects of Mephistopheles and his underworld minions reveal themselves in flexible motifs and exquisite instrumentation; there is broad humour in much of the choral writing, the students' 'blasphemous' rendering of an ecclesiastic fugue, and hellish language invented by Berlioz for fearsome incantation. The ballad of the King of Thule has an unworldly medieval feeling, a pathetic tale reminiscing on the death of a young Queen, used as a portent of Marguerite's fate.

In 1869, Gounod expanded his work into a grand opera, recitative replacing spoken dialogue, with an additional act and ballet sequence set in Ancient Greece. Yet the treatment virtually ignored the philosophical aspects so important in the original drama, and its critics have always accused Gounod of trivialisation. Many burlesques soon appeared in London and Paris, and within one year, Hervé had provided his own, called *Petit Faust*, a reduction of the story and its characters to the absurd. He includes galops for the 'underworld' creatures, comic songs for Mephisto, and parodies of famous scenes in Gounod.

■ ■ ■

Petit Faust opens in Faust's Academy, a large, gloomy room, to be illuminated by the great man's intellect; but the atmosphere is more suited to the permissive 1990s than the severe 1870s. Faust has a shrill voice, arriving to quell a riot by confronting Siebel, the chief trouble-maker:

So you think you are a man? Prove it.

This is an insolent youth, in contrast to Gounod's gentle Siebel who has suffered unrequited love for Marguerite. He is played as in Gounod by a soprano, so Faust's challenge is declined. The professor is further provoked by a girl's indifference to the classical education on offer, and croaks his way through a cantilena before stumbling badly at a coloratura passage. He boasts that, at the age of 70, he is still 'pure' and regards love as no more than a dictionary definition.

Lessons are interrupted by the first nine notes of Gounod's famous march, to which Hervé tacks on his own very confident chorus. Valentin has arrived with his soldiers, to say he is off to war though really to dump his sister onto the school. So the first encounter between Faust and Marguerite breaks tradition by being academic, though very loosely. To those familiar with the opening of Goethe's play, it is no surprise that Faust asks if she qualifies with a knowledge of Theology, Philosophy and Medicine. She does not!!

She sings *The Flower of Innocence* with conviction, enough to be accepted, then behaves like a delinquent and promptly qualifies for corporal punishment, a collective ritual in this establishment. The comments on Hervé's performance as Faust by Emily Soldene are quaintly suggestive:

> 'Such girls – every size, sort, shape – so pretty: you should have heard and seen the school-room scene, such chatter, chatter. And what a high old time did that arch imposter Faust have when we all went up for 'two slaps' for insubordination, telling a funny story, and other iniquities.'

Mephisto is a splendid pantomime figure, with feminine shape, voice and allure, arriving to a cymbal stroke. To provide Faust with all he desires, just one evil deed from him is necessary, and that is not specified.

She transports him to a cafe-concert of the less reputable kind, and Act II begins with some high kicking at Paris' famed Bal Mabille. Here the women of the *demi-monde* provide the attractions, some selling flowers as a cover. There is a curious reversal between the young and old men's priorities, the veterans fascinated by the movements of the dancers' breasts whilst the students just want a smoke. Complaints that the King spends their taxes on his mistresses induces Mephisto to sing *The Song of the Flea*, disrespectful of pomp and royalty.

Rejuvenated by Mephisto's magic, Faust is now a light tenor, romanticing about his visits to Europe's capitals where his 'blood was whipped-up'; but he is pining for the elusive Marguerite. All the Marguerites of the world are commanded to appear, chorus lines dancing through in changing colours to a rapid valse tempo, an international parade of melody with popular songs such as *The Carnival of Venice*. *God Save the Queen* is played as if it were the most boring anthem in Europe, specially when Faust joins in, and the Germans respond with Hervé's oom-pa-pa *Fatherland song.*

This is a perverse story, and with perspectives changing or rapidly falsified, even nationalities are uncertain. Marguerite's voice deepens alarmingly when she calls herself 'Gretchen' and sings a Tyrolean ditty, but Faust is enthralled. He has become a pathological liar, and though speaking no German, claims to be 'Deutsch' through his father, so passing himself off as his own son.

At the Bal Mabille, he is assailed by delusions of horror when he thinks he is in a Gothic castle, no place for an innocent girl! So he kidnaps Marguerite, meets up and quarrels with her brother, who, as tradition demands, is run through by Faust's sword with Mephisto's help. In this version, she throws snuff in Valentin's face. He takes a long, long time to die, sufficient for a mini-cantata to see him off, and to realise that he was not felled by a tobacconist. He knows his foe, and rest assured, will return.

The wedding feast. Marguerite obliges with a ballad less refined than it sounds, about a King of Thune who reveals public secrets at an official function when his pants fall down. Dignity is restored with some majestic notes from *Lohengrin*. To shimmering Wagnerian strings, the bridal couple are about to taste the soup when out pops the ghost of Valentin from the bowl.

'Assassin' is an alarming hiss in French, and to chilling groans, Faust shapes up like Macbeth at the banquet, suffering guilt-ridden visions. Like Lady Macbeth, Gretchen presses on with the celebrations to military accompaniment and a compelling choral monotone.

Retribution follows swiftly. Faust has fulfilled his contracted crime, but so late in the day that he must now submit to the Devil's will. The party's over, and if Marguerite is to be saved, she must be transformed into a genuine operatic heroine. Her glorious passage to Heaven in Gounod's version, combines drama with the religious intensity of oratorio. Berlioz despatches Faust to Hell in a terrifying journey to relentless driving rhythms. How shall our Hervé match these enthralling scenes?

Heroic sentiments, not yet apparent in *Petit Faust*, accompany Valentin who is heaven-bound, and his sister's soaring melody brings hope that she is to be saved. Faust clings on to her, hoping a joint passport will suffice, but she cannot sustain the emotions of grand opera, and an unholy galop seizes her.

For better or worse, the couple are launched together, and Hell is the destination. Installed as the Prince of Darkness, Mephisto is in commanding voice as the lovers, along with the habitués of the Bal Mabille, take to the floor in a frantic knees-up. Hell is an unending dance.

■　■　■

Gounod would not have attended this work, and Berlioz was spared it, having died some years before. Meyerbeer liked this kind of fun, though as a German, he had refused to conduct Gounod's *Faust*, seeing it as an insult to the original classic.

Wagner's stage humour was quite heavy-handed, but he specially enjoyed Hervé's clowning at the piano and his stage works, commenting that 'Hervé is the man who has impressed me most favourably in Paris.' This remark should be set against Wagner's known hostility to the V.I.P.s of the city's opera, perhaps implying that French music theatre is best fitted for laughter.

In 1880, the *Faust* burlesque appeared in an expanded English version, *Mephisto II*. London's taste for Hervé and Gothic scenarios was good reason to place Faust back in his German home on the mountainous Brocken where, according to popular superstition, on *Walpurgis* night (May the first), witches ride on broomsticks and obscene revelries occur.

In Goethe's drama, this scene is intended to evoke the pagan spirit, along with the image of Ancient Greece. Mephistopheles takes Faust on a journey through time, conjuring up visions calculated to excite in a Classics scholar both passion and imagination. For Faust, the ultimate human experience is to love and procreate with Helen of Troy.

Arrigo Boito's *Mefistofele (1868)* gave the aesthetic and metaphysical aspects of Goethe's work most imaginative treatment, and Faust is elevated to an heroic level. Only Mephistophclcs is bored with the visions of classical beauty and longs for the orgies of *Walpurgis* night.

These sophisticated elaborations of a legend could be an excellent target for burlesque, far more than the Marguerite story, and when the opera reached London in 1880, it led to the Hervé revision. The critic of the *Era* looked much further for allusions and likened the music accompanying Faust's temptation on the Brocken to the *pas de fascination* in *Robert le Diable*. Not surprisingly, he concluded that brief excerpts from Felix Mendelssohn's *Walpurgis* Cantata did not fit well with the rest of the score.

Hervé, a cart-load of tricks and 'One in the Eye'

4 Tales of Offenbach

Offenbach composed two of the world's best-known melodies, but that does not explain why today his stage works are so widely and increasingly performed. He wrote more musicals than any other composer of comparable ability, and for the uninitiated, seeing one of them the first time in the dignity of an opera house might be a culture shock.

No such inhibition affected a gathering of fairly young revellers in the stalls of the London Coliseum one evening around 1980. They knew their man, and a certain musical about Helen of Troy, and were ready for the bacchanal. Among the stalls there was some dancing in the aisles, quite appropriately; as the historical review of the first century of French operetta commented:

Genuine operettas have finales which eject viewers from their seats, fizzing choruses that make heads spin.

This London 'office party' must have created an ambiance like that among the Parisians who attended the first entertainment given at Offenbach's tiny theatre, opened in the Champs Elysées during the 1855 International Exhibition. On the opening night at that theatre, a new item in a triple bill was dramatically a very small firework with a big impact. At 36, Offenbach was ready to challenge Paris, starting with a risky theme of two 'blind', greedy beggars.

Because of the severe poverty of the '50s, some of his backers warned against what we would now call political incorrectness. Yet villains are everywhere, and audiences gave enthusiastic approval to the farce that started with a melody which might suggest a sturdy beggar and included one in the mock-pathetic music hall style. These and other tunes fast became Parisian street-songs.

Jacques Offenbach had been poor for too long to sentimentalise about it; a Rhineland Jew, he had arrived in Paris aged 14, with his older brother, to study at the Conservatoire.

The pair had nothing to survive on except musical talent. Jacques would perform as cellist at concerts even where payment was a kind of charity and success was helped by his natural wit and charm. His appearance was bird-like, quick and elusive, eager to fly off on his cello; he was described as a cross between a cock and a grass-hopper. He had a rare gift for imitation, often of the most curious sounds, as if he was playing every instrument but his own.

During the 1840s, Jacques composed popular pieces, mainly ballads, valses and other dances easily sold, but he did not welcome a virtuoso's life and a sense of destiny that he should create in the theatre left him frustrated. The first break was appointment as musical director at the Comédie-Française where he composed the incidental music, and had almost a free hand to improve standards during the early 1850s. A promising musical was *Pepito (1853)*, built around a fop who imagines he is as wily as Figaro. After a boastful *Factotum* aria which is close to Rossini's, his plans for a seduction collapse in full view. The intended victim, Offenbach's first señorita, seems as formidable as his later heroines:

> SHE: *If you try that again, I'l slap you till your teeth rattle like castanets.*
> HE: *This is no time for a discussion of percussion.*

The work was well received in Germany, and a leading Rhineland paper expressed the hope that their favoured son would storm the Paris opera. Meanwhile, he could only give private showings in Paris, having to sing the Rossini parody.

Given his vocal inadequacy, that might have sounded very funny; but for his next project, he would at least look the part. This was the story of a double-bass player captured by a cannibal queen who desires him gastronomically. Like Scheherazade, he keeps her at bay with the charm of his muse, but unlike her, escapes down-river on his instrument.

He never acted in a commercial performance, but Hervé was ideal to play and sing the hungry lady's role when producing this work, *The Queen of the Isles (1855)*. Offenbach learned much from this brief collaboration, but was envious that Hervé, who did not share his entry to the fashionable salons, had his own theatre. Yet even before the cannibal farce's run ended, Offenbach was to have his own venue, where he was permitted as many as four singers. In this, he was helped by the Duc de Morny, the Emperor's half-brother and political fixer who took an active interest in the work of Offenbach and Hervé. He was specially keen for the public to be distracted by frivolities, leaving the privileged to explore the numerous ways of making money. He thought it fair play if such practices were satirised.

Following *The two blind Men*, *A Mid-summer Night's Dream (1855)* found another easy target, ridiculing the English as lovers. It pays scant respect to Shakespeare, and features two absurd Englishmen saying 'Very good' to everything Parisian, and competing for one woman at the disreputable Bal Mabille ... where else?

Offenbach's theatre would be pulled down like the rest of the Exhibition site. The new Bouffes Parisiens was not so cramped, and he remained in charge for nearly ten years before trying mixed fortunes as impresario at larger theatres. From 1855 to 1857, he was composing a new stage work at the rate of more than one every two months, with a commitment to establish a genre of opera *bouffe* to contrast with the 'heavier' works seen at the Opera-Comique, where, he argued, inferior music was being hidden behind a facade of large orchestral and theatrical effects; the comparison he made was with women's crinolines.

Young composers were encouraged, and for them he organised a competition in which they all had to compose to a farcical text, *Doctor Miracle*. It was judged by a distinguished jury and won jointly by Georges Bizet, his future friend, and Charles Lecocq, his future enemy. Both operettas were a failure on being performed at the Bouffes; there is no substitute for hard theatre experience.

Offenbach unearthed a farce by his beloved Mozart, *The Impresario*, consisting largely of a musical slanging match between two prima donnas. For a time, he was set on outright slap-stick, and two idiosyncratic works which deflate heroic plots are the most likely from the years before 1858 to be performed today.

Ba-Ta-Clan is a surreal threesome in Italo-Chinese gibberish, setting off with a chorale which sounds like Meyerbeer in his noblest style, but a frantic escape drama is soon underway.

Dynamo-propelled vocal gymnastics and a grotesque 'eastern' fanfare, at the climax a battle-edged version of Martin Luther's revered hymn[1]: the Reformation and grand opera turned into an 'oriental' farce.

The Act V finale to Meyerbeer's *Huguenots* was a dramatisation of the massacre of Huguenots on St Barthomew's Day in the Paris of 1572. Its close parody in *Ba-Ta-Clan* is to the French a slice of black humour; but why should Chinese dignitaries intone Luther's name and dance a cancan? They are soon exposed as Parisians in disguise.

In contrast to these strident convulsions, *Croquefer* (Ironmug), deploys similar resources for gentle strumming and tooting, a tale of medieval chivalry which used Hervé's tricks to overcome the legal limit on singers. *Croquefer's* battle-scarred enemy is dumb, and staggers about on one leg, carrying the accoutrements of war and a board where he writes military commands and incidental banalities. By the time the theatre restrictions ended, the stunt was too popular to be discarded, though the much-challenged hero is permitted to join in a final quintet after rescuing his long-lost daughter.

Audiences expected witty asides, from the vaudeville tradition, and enjoyed history flavoured with anachronisms. This heroine helps herself to half the great love duet from *The Huguenots*, then is seized by a desire to attend the Opera Ball. In return, she condescends to publicise a great institution:

> *The Opera is a temple where virtue is rewarded, and everything is illuminated by wit and good taste … a paradise where for six francs a time even the dancing is respectable enough for mothers to take their daughters.*

When Offenbach went beyond mockery in *The Devil's Three Kisses (also 1857)*, the music disconcerted some of his audience, and he did not exploit his more sinister powers fully until his last opera, *The Tales of Hofmann*. At the other extreme, *The Cat turned into Woman (1858)* with its *Miaow* song, was an addition to the repertoire of the musical menagerie, to which Rossini, Saint-Saens and Prokofief have also contributed.[2]

Among the one-acters, the most intensive operatic send-up arrived in 1861 to a text written anonymously by Morny,

Mr Cauliflower's Party. The host, a *nouveau-riche* greengrocer, plans to impress associates with a divertissement from Rossini to Verdi, hopefully presented by the finest singers of the Paris Opera. His daughter is 'very advanced' for her age, especially when deceiving the father about her secret lover, a poor musician who would not be thought eligible by any 'respectable' parents. She sings several familiar melodies from a past age: a Mozart aria, a nursery rhyme[3], and *Plaisir d'amour*, the earliest French romance still to be known world-wide. The young man creeps in, then with papa absent, can stamp his feet to *macho* flamenco dance.

The party is about to start, but the singers fail to arrive and poor Mr Cauliflower is forced to acknowledge the boy-friend as together they conspire to put on a show. The three of them carry-out the impersonations in a sequence of arias exploiting the conventions and stilted language of Italian opera. There are parodies of a languid Bellini love duet, the quartet from *Rigoletto* and an accelerating Rossini ensemble.

By the time theatres were free to stage much larger productions, Offenbach had a bundle of tricks to include in his first use of a full chorus. The tear-away opening to *The Ladies of la Halle (1858)* incongruously mixes liturgical strains, choirboys, and a rowdy catalogue of street hawkers. This farrago issuing from Paris' famous market is hyped up to operatic grandeur during an absurdly prolonged recognition scene[4], with everyone in sight being identified. The voices of two men in drag add to the confusion.

A horseman in warlike declamation weighs in, and a drum-major suitably named Raflafla renders a storming recruiting song, a *rataplan*[5]. Tensions are relieved by a swinging dance, not too fast for the elders to join in, the first Offenbach chorus to become a 'hit'.

Over decades, his private musical evenings favoured a 'collaborative' approach to musical farces: at one fancy dress party Georges Bizet came clothed as a baby, and in an improvised poultry-yard symphony, Delibes impersonated an angry dog. Comic ideas and routines were developed which would eventually confront Parisian theatre audiences as never before, and on the largest stages.

By far the most ambitious venture to that time was to turn the classic love story of *Orpheus and Eurydice* on its head.

Offenbach's librettists devised a plot where both partners welcome Eurydice's being seduced and carried off to Hades by Pluto. A most effective innovation was to replace the Greek chorus with a female persona, Public Opinion, who breaks in to demand that in the interests of decency, Orpheus must express the deepest regret at the loss of his wife, and appeal to Jupiter and the gods for restitution. There is no resistance, and from this point, Public Opinion is wielded as an intrusive satirical device.

An opera *bouffe*, *Orpheus in the Underworld*, started as a tightly-constructed two-acter, amplified with many soloists, large chorus and double-sized orchestra. The public could not see enough of the gods in carnival mood, and with its certainty as a money-spinner, *Orpheus* was steadily expanded over 16 years into a sprawling 4-hour song-and-dance show.

It is now generally staged in a cut-down version without the costly ballet additions of the 1874 production, when Offenbach impudently celebrated the centenary of the Paris version of Gluck's *Orpheus and Eurydice*. Already in 1858, he had taken from that tragic masterpiece Orpheus' love song, *Che farò* (What is life to me?), using it mockingly as a violin solo in the midst of the final dance orgy. That shocked some purists.

In modern productions, the action conveniently fits into three acts: the earth-bound seduction and Public Opinion's intervention; Orpheus' journey to Mount Olympus, the disputes among the gods, and the summoning of Pluto; the whole assembly descending to Hades, ostensibly to resolve the Euridice dispute, but because Heaven is boring, actually to have a party.

An 1874 addition was a fourth act in which Pluto is put on trial for abducting Eurydice, with the triple-headed dog, Cerberus[6] giving witness, a growling trio in surly monosyllables. This buffoonery was neatly included in the classic Sadlers Wells- E.N.O. version which lasted a quarter of a century before being replaced in 1986 by one in most ways inferior.

Offenbach did not write long overtures, and the 'concert' version known today was not arranged by him. It presents some of the finest melodies, such as one suggesting Eurydice's pleasurable anticipation of a new love affair. Is the arresting violin theme from Orpheus' Concerto opus 1, with its extreme sweetness, dropping a sly hint that Eurydice has good reason to say she detests it? The Overture's moments of 'hellish' ballet music suggests the dances Gounod composed for his *Faust*. With Offenbach, nothing need be quite what it seems.

In at least one recent production, the orchestra strikes up the Overture, but almost immediately, Public Opinion appears, telling them to 'shut-up' so that the real action can start. The composer would have enjoyed this addition, and *Orpheus*, with its spoof of a great legend, was to be a sophisticated exercise in breaking the conventions, the prototype of the large-scale classical operetta, and an immense advance in the history of the musical.

One anecdote among the Offenbach legends is that when he first interviewed a future vedette, Lise Tautin, she sang a Moorish song so dirge-like that he immediately shifted it on the piano to a major key, accelerated and composed what in *Orpheus* became the 'infernal galop'. The three most accented notes at the opening, *doh, re, soh* form a motif which runs through the whole score. This is the kind of ingenuity in thematic transformation which one finds in a few great operettas, such as *Die Fledermaus*, and in many operas.

The motif is also apparent within (first two notes repeated) the most assertive phrase of the *Marseillaise: (Allons, en) -fants de la pa-trie* . . . and that symbol of revolution is woven into the musical score at the height of the gods' 'political' protest.

The three-note motif is present in other fine melodies, such as *John Styx's* (Boethian King's) aria, the only 'sentimental' moment in a facetious score, and when Diana taunts Jupiter's about the metamorphoses[7] which he uses to further his promiscuous sex-life. Once in Hades, he displays this skill, turning himself into a fly in order to touch Eurydice's body whilst she bathes and he hums and buzzes to Offenbach's funniest insect song. The interplay of her disarming innocence and his disguised naughtiness made for a piquant scene, with 1860s' audiences thinking of the Emperor's taste for young women.

The unexpected often breaks up solemn occasions or the anticipated dance movements, such as Mercury's 'knees-up' galop, now often presented with space-age imagery, and the one leisurely moment at the Hades party when guests dance a minuet, before leaping into the frenetic chorus. This finale became the model for those in his following compositions, the breath-taking sequences of tempi which create the illusion of permanent acceleration, *Offenbachiades.*

The 'infernal galop' was among the first of many Offenbach specialities to receive popular, if not vulgar exploitation by others. It rapidly transferred to French and other music halls, girl dancers jumping in with abandonment and ending with the splits, the definitive form of a 'disreputable' dance of Moroccan origin, the cancan. Though this piece will certainly remain as an irresistible cabaret spectacle world-wide for another century and a half, that elemental *Orpheus* melody is just one of a hundred galops or cancans by Offenbach, musically interesting whilst permitting female thighs to be equally visible. Many of these have been recorded in the popular orchestral suite, once arranged for the Monte Carlo ballet, *Gaîté Parisienne.*

Orpheus was to be followed by satirical treatment of another historic theme, Charles Martel and the Franks, who 'saved Europe from the Saracens' by defeating them at Tours in AD 732. This mock-epic, *Genevieve of Brabant (1859),* is centred on the legend of a Duchess deprived through court intrigue of her conjugal rights and almost of her life. The villain, Golo, has contrived to keep the Duke so busy that he has no energy to produce an heir; Golo plans to kill the master, succeed as court favourite to the title and marry Genevieve.

The Duke is presented as a *buffo* character, his libido restored by a pastry full of vitamins, and he celebrates with a cockerel song which propels him into a cancan. The course of love is interrupted by the arrival of Charles Martel who orders the Duke to accompany him on a crusade.

The youthful pastry-cook asks as a reward to be made page to the Duchess whom of course he adores. Before the Duke departs, Golo frames the couple, and she is condemned; this leads to a stormy finale led by Charles Martel's *From head to toe I'm armed.*

Genevieve is to be left as Golo's prisoner but flees to the forest with her new page; this is a soprano role, and they sound throughout like a loving pair. The crusaders never leave France, at Narbonne rain stops play and they are diverted to Asnières where they proceed to enjoy energetic dancing and wenching. The finale is festive and exuberant, resembling the one which accompanies the gods from Olympus to Hades in the second finale of *Orpheus*.

Chronology is treated very freely, the centuries being spanned by the appearance of such notables as Saladin and Don Quixote, accompanied by the medieval farandole, more timely than a *tyrolienne*. To complaisant music, the Duke enjoys adultery with an unknown lady, who is later revealed as the formidable wife of Golo. He in the final reckoning is handed over for her vengeance.

The prodigious Asnières act was omitted from the first unsatisfactory London version, either because of the cost or its sweeping ridicule of Christian endeavour. In contrast, Offenbach was driven by the lively story line to spend a fortune during the '70s expanding *Genevieve* into the ultimate 5-act spectacular. Yet despite the level of inspiration, unlike *Orpheus* it is rarely heard now, except for two specially funny numbers which are widely performed out of context.

Prior to dismissing the treasonable Golo, the Duke returns home from Asnières in disguise, with a stomping patter song, *Je viens de la Turque, j'en fiche de la Turque* (I come from Turkey, to hell with Turkey). A subsidiary theme about corrupt officialdom is best remembered in English for the song about the gendarmes who 'turn in ... those that do no harm'. This stirring tune is now the regimental march of the U.S. Marines, *To the Shores of Tripoli*.

Purpose-written romantic ballets of one to two hours' duration have become the norm in the 20th century but were almost an innovation in 1861 when Offenbach decided to 'do' for traditional ballet what Orpheus had 'done' for Greek myths. To some balletomanes, the treatment was an attack on the dignity and beauty of their art. Its theme was romance and magic gone wrong, with the participants suffering loss of integrity, shape or youth. For what could have been a gossamer tale, he composed some disconcerting music and scenes richly melodic in bel canto style, sometimes introduced by a mysterious rising motif.

Early-Romantic trappings include Weber-like horn passages and fairy music; but he also added much strident orchestral music which suggested the wilder rhythms of peasants and of central Europe: an open-air atmosphere rather than ballroom. This was a valuable trend which would become increasingly familiar in Western countries during the following decades.

In the world of ballet, the effect was to please most of the public, enthral novelist Gustav Flaubert, but infuriate the critics and purists, such as those who regarded as a high point in the emergence of Romantic ballet, *Giselle (1841)*, which was obviously being pilloried.

Thematic transformation continues to enrich the orchestral score. That rising motif which can shimmer in an ultra-Romantic glow elsewhere emerges as a thumping parody of a mazurka rhythm, so instantly attractive that within a year or two, it had even been transported to London as a popular 'English' song. In this guise, with melody and rhythm slightly modified to a less interesting sound, it was still widely known a century later as 'The daring young man on a flying trapeze.'

Papillon's Valse des rayons, a dance with several fine melodies in the grand manner of Johann Strauss' *Emperor Waltz*, had a gently whirling theme of much distinction. This was adapted (1912), given a passionate *macho* rhythm and choreography, suggesting Parisian low-life, to achieve independent fame; it is still performed in revues in its adapted form as the *Apaché Dance*.

Papillon was Offenbach's unique full-length ballet. Yet it was virtually to disappear from the stage, to the satisfaction of those who were offended by it; when Emma Livry, a distinguished young ballerina associated with it, was burnt to death performing in opera, popular superstition played its part.

When the doors of the Opera-Comique were finally opened to him, he could not resist one jest too many. *Barkouf* (1860) featured a dog with a very limited musical vocabulary, and audiences were not amused. Hector Berlioz wrote that it was as licentious as Caligula making his horse a senator; for these and other observations, Berlioz was ridiculed in a short stage work, with a band which reached to kitchen utensils. Its title was *Mr Bassoon*, which was not intended as a tribute to his unique wood-wind writing, the bassoon being held among musicians as a comic instrument. Offenbach was offended that his early advocacy of Berlioz had not been returned, but continued to study avidly his treatise on orchestration.

The Bridge of Sighs (1861) was a carnival romp which pillories men seasonally or otherwise obsessed with infidelity. Except for that aspect, much of its plot was closely parallelled by Gilbert's *Gondoliers (1887)*. Similarities of treatment by Sullivan, notably in adapting 'Venetian' rhythms, are striking, but the differences equally so; Offenbach music is licentious and Sullivan's not at all.

The Bridge of Sighs is easily enjoyed without knowing that it is parodying the lighter forms of French opera, especially of the earlier 19th century. Into a diatribe about money, a steely version of the song of revolt from Auber's *Masaniello* is introduced. Offenbach rarely used another composer's melody in its entirety, but this one had created perhaps the most extraordinary effect in all opera. One performance had inspired a riot which lead to Belgian independence in 1830.

Offenbach intended to succeed with grand opera but first suffered a setback. *The Rhine Fairies (1864)* wandered into German Romanticism, almost into Wagner territory, but he could never treat such a theme seriously and he wasted much good material, but saving a fine valse to become the Barcarolle in *Hofmann*.

Wagner would have expressed the event more crudely; he was appalled that this operatic 'trifle' had been given priority over his own *Tristan* in Vienna. During the 1861 Paris visit, Offenbach had criticised his whole aesthetic, and composed a short send-up, *The Musician of the Future*, not a very good or subtle work; but it was enough. He considered including a parody of a *Tannhäuser* scene in his projected story of Helen of Troy, but decided against it; the animosity between the two men had gone too far for more humour.

It had been fanned at an international level. Germans who had turned against Wagner, such as the great critic Hanslick, set up Offenbach as a model. Friedrich Nietzsche wrote that his music was:

> ... 'imbued with Voltaire's intellect almost to the point of banality, free from the fragrance of morbid Viennese sensuality. Wagner is heavy and clumsy; there is nothing so remote to him as the moments of wanton perfection which

this clown Offenbach achieves half a dozen times in nearly every one of his buffooneries.'

The Georgian Ladies was designed to match *Genevieve of Brabant* as a spectacular opera-*bouffe*, featuring 'elephants' on stage. The story derived from the popular notion that the women of that country are specially passionate. A certain pasha, Turkish of course, hears of this, and decides that by making war, he could seize enough of them to last a lifetime. He emulates Hannibal's feat in leading his animals over mountains, this time the Caucasian Alps.[8]

The Georgian males flee, returning with self-inflicted wounds in time for the Act I Finale, so the women are driven to desperate remedies. They train as Amazons, equipped with their own *Marseillaise*, defeat and capture the Pasha, who in chains is forced to play the big drum in the women's victory parade.

The Parisian males were most impressed by this exciting display of feminine might, necessitating a more scanty form of dress, with at least one bare breast. Hervé was similarly impressed, introducing Amazons onto his stage a few years later.

Offenbach was entering the decade of extraordinary successes, and several followed before his second composition of undisputed genius in 1864, *La Belle Hélène* (Helen), a send-up of the *Iliad* and Paris' abduction of Helen. She feels no remorse about her fated infidelity to husband, King Menelaus, because she is the plaything of the gods, especially of the love goddess, Venus. Awaiting her future lover, Paris, who will be bearing an apple, brings her to an ecstatic state; one could not call him 'the Apple Man' in English, but in French, the repetition of '*L'Homme à la pomme*' builds up its own momentum into a very funny coloratura aria. With Paris slipping into her bedroom, she decides to face seduction as if it were 'all a dream', and they sing a duet to a swooning waltz.

Contemporaneous references struck home. There is a board game covering most of the stage, suggesting diversions played by the actual French court, and talk of Venus sending her special illness to Paris, not the prince but the town; an epidemic of venereal disease struck during the 1860s. Fortunately, the Emperor laughed as much as anyone,

Offenbach having been accepted as informal court jester. The state religion is to be satirised; high priest, Calchas, is a comic figure, a politician adept at sharp dealings, and an image-maker.

A 'grand entry of the kings' is a devastating operatic parody, in which several heroes of the *Iliad* are reduced to their most absurd posturing. Achilles sings about his heel and King Ajax, who had a bad press in the *Iliad*, is compensated with two personae, Ajax A and Ajax B, a bass and a tenor, generally large and small. The courtiers are curious to know who is hiding behind a distinguished beard:

> *This beard, do guess who's behind it, guess who's behind it, guess who's behind it – Agamemnon Rex.*
> *I quite expressly designed it, 'pressly designed it, 'pressly designed it, for the fairer sex.*

Later, they dance a 'patriotic trio' to a theme borrowed from Rossini's *William Tell*, once composed to great acclaim for the Paris opera.

King Menelaus is turned into a buffoon, with the distinction of becoming one of the most celebrated cuckolds in history - or literature:

> *The bureaucrat Menelaus, rat Menelaus, rat Menelaus, heav'nly Helen's mate,*
> *Our wives agree to obey us, 'gree to obey us,' gree to obey us, then they deviate.*

For several minutes he has centre stage, asking in croaking recitative:

> *What have they done with my good name? . . . And is it quite fair?*

The court accept this declaration with mock solemnity, a grand tableau in the Rossini manner, the principals remaining statuesque, repeating the words in turn but with the ensemble rising to a crescendo of derision, until Helen breaks the tension with a cool offer, to general consent, that she will share the blame:

> *A husband who has gone away, proposes to come home one day,*
> *It's prudent then if he contrive to send word when he will arrive*
> . . .

The climax reveals Paris finally making-off by boat with

Helen for Venus' island, Cytheria, disguised and in grotesque falsetto voice as Venus' augurer. For the first authentic English-language version in a London production, the difficulty of this role was partly overcome by employing a 'principal girl' mezzo, but normally Paris is a lyric tenor. The final coup is a choral build-up in accelerating tempo, their acceptance of Venus' command merging seamlessly into a sweeping version of the waltz-dream melody.

By 1866, these stage works were having a broad social effect in Paris far beyond the music, relating to fashion and language, in this area just as broadcast shows in more recent times have influenced verbal humour. Yet in the England of the 1860s, burlesques in smaller theatres and music halls which had been satisfactory for Offenbach's early trifles did no justice for these increasingly sophisticated works. *Helen* arrived only after 5 years when the *Era* thought the English would not take to satire of classical legends, but would find the music irresistible.

No such problems affected a later work, *The Grand Duchess*, which arrived in London a few months after Paris (1867), reaching other capitals, and crossing the Atlantic in similar time. Such far-reaching success was unprecedented for an opera and this most rampant of scores put the work in top place, its musical treatment being very different from *Helen*, a 'military' opera, more marches and galops, this time with bells on.

One Offenbach joke has generally escaped detection, though it relates to one of the best known of the military songs. Expressing great love for her soldiers, the Grand Duchess jumps after two notes into the invigorating melody, which with slight rhythmic variation opens the finale to Beethoven's 7th Symphony.

War and diplomacy are satirised, with an insight that was to prove too close for comfort in the unfolding 1860s. The Emperor saw the worst-ever recorded carnage at Magenta, Italy, in 1859 but shortly before, his vacuous wife had spoken of young men 'enjoying war'. As the Grand Duchess was just as obtuse, she was to be 'distanced' from France.

She takes a fancy to a young private, who is consequently promoted, taking over from General Boum as Commander-in-Chief, and becoming the play's unwitting hero. When he refuses to leave his peasant fiancée, he is reduced to the ranks; Catherine the Great's inclination to have her lovers murdered in quick time might have been suggested by the activities of this stage Grand Duchess. So in order to avoid offending the Russian Tsar – who was scheduled to see the work in Paris – the Duchess was to be accredited to a mythical German state, Gerolstein.

Boum is slow-witted, bombastic and incompetent, and his theme-song, *Piff-paff-puff*, would have raised an extra laugh in Paris, having taken its title from an ouburst by a militant Protestant in *Les Huguenots*. Buffetted even in the debased world of court intrigue, Boum stands as an outsize *buffo* role.

At the height of the 1914–18 war, a Berlin production found every good reason to present the Grand Duchess as a feudal Russian tyrant. The Germans (and later East Germans) have tended to favour this work whilst inserting a more modern plot, bringing from abroad an actress as an impostor, in order to effect a *coup d'état*.

Blue-beard is a spoof in which the legendary lady-killer with his bouncy theme-song is made more comic than villain, to be tamed by a peasant-girl. When presented at palace, she thinks it her duty to offer herself to the leading dignitaries, and when she throws herself upon the King who is in a state of senile decay, the uncouth couple are ejected. She is not altogether to blame, having just witnessed at the madcap court a sequence of incoherent conversations.

The Grand Duchess was the fourth collaboration – nine in all – between librettists, Ludovic Halévy and Henri Meilhac. Their third is in many ways considered Offenbach's most characteristic work, a warm musical tribute to his adopted city. *La Vie Parisienne* was a comedy of Paris in the times of the great international exhibitions, the rich visitors and the professional scroungers. Two of these plan to gratify at a price a Swedish baron with forbidden pleasures, and to divert his wife with whatever she wishes.

As in classic farce, humour is derived from most participants busily pretending to be what they are not, and to complete their deceits, many sing plausible if eccentric songs. When a 'Swiss admiral's' uniform splits down the back, the ensemble offer advice in the style of traditional oratorio. A 'dowager' expresses alternate grief and pleasure at her husband's departure. A banquet's formalities are attended by a ludicrous yodelling song. In more sentimental style, a love duet permits some enchanting vocal intimacy, and there is a nimble evocation of *Frou-Frou*.

Offenbach was ready with another opera-comique. *Robinson Crusoe* opens in the style of a bourgeois comedy; the prodigal son, Robinson, has a sententious father who expresses himself in four-square melody, whilst the three women of the household praise his erring son with the ironical *Oh, what a charming boy*.

Robinson is the romantic tenor, in his dreams secure from fearful adversity and never indulging in the musical antics of his companions. After ten years' absence from home, he has to be advised of the changed social scene in a catchy patter-song, each syllable accentuated, which in one translation matches Britain of the 1990s:

> *There's no place like England, We're taught so in schools,*
> *We once ruled the waves, Now we just waive the rules . . .*
> *The British are friendly, reserved and sincere,*
> *If you're being murdered they won't interfere . . .*
> *The British are sportsmen, It's best in their view*
> *To be a good loser . . . so that's all they do.*

Man Friday is a mezzo role, uninhibited and musically odd in contrast to Robinson. Pirates and savages are faced, but the rising tension which prepares Crusoe's fiancée for ritual sacrifice to the Sun-god is suspended with the help of European culture as she sweeps the natives into a huge waltz. A furious duet for the young married couple, *I wish I'd never married you*, is a galop almost too fast to dance.

Crusoe was a modest success in a new direction which *La Perichole* was to follow also in 1868, based on a true story of a wandering girl's affair with a Viceroy of Peru. Highlights include a colourful parody of a Verdi court scene[9], one of the finest operatic letter songs and a sing-along chorus asserting that *All Spaniards know the ways of love*.

During the 1850s, a Comte de Tascher used to entertain the Imperial court with bird and animal impersonations. He might have been commemorated in *The Island of Tulipatan (1868)*, where at the whim of a mad Duke, courtiers are drilled into imitating ducks, waddling past him in single file.

As he could not produce male heirs, his youngest daughter has been brought up thinking she is a man. His prime minister, anxious that his only son should avoid conscription, has turned him into a girl, but one with a curious love of military noises which he spends his leisure reproducing on brass instruments. Complications arise when the young couple want to get married.

This is a shorter work which is appearing in the foyers of opera houses today, and with its scope for innovative lunacies, is becoming popular with amateur operatic societies.

The moral of *The Brigands (1869)* is that political leaders commit fraud like any gang-leader, a condition exemplified by certain statesmen and women even in our enlightened times. An official party from Granada is waylaid by bandits en route to Mantua. They display in exaggerated style the gestures and rhythms of Spain's traditional musical, the *zarzuela*. The commanding señorita on pantomime horse is subjected, along with her party, to losing her dignity and her clothes. The same treatment is handed-out to the Italian *carabinieri*, grossly incompetent but given a famous tramping chorus.

Vert-Vert (1869) is probably the best Offenbach operetta to have failed in England, though it is not clear how much of its authentic version was seen at the St James' theatre in 1874 where it was said to be a disgraceful counterfeit. When its so-called *reperelle* was described as the most indecent dance in London, the impresario, a Mr Fairlie, took a libel suit to the High Court, ending up with a large solicitors' bill probably more than covered by added box office returns.

Vert-Vert was a parrot but this was not another Offenbach venture into the animal world, nor was it required to sing, having died before the start of the play. It is sent off by the school where it was a pet and to a funeral march. A young man assumes the nick-name in hopes of gaining the affection of those girls at the local seminary.

There is a fine Romance with the music well suited to a French bedroom farce, in this case the intrigue arising from three inmates having secretly married. The Overture is distinguished by the fizzing theme of the first act finale followed by the dragoons' march which prances astonishingly down-up-down the scale, suggesting horse-play of males in forbidden places.

One woman is often the commanding personality in this developing style of operetta, and sopranos of star quality became an essential for leading musicals. Hortense Schneider presumably had more sex appeal than natural beauty, but was a good natural singer, handling gesture and innuendo superbly. She was closely associated with Helen, the Grand Duchess and other roles, whilst artistes, such as Anna Judic, moved between Offenbach and Hervé shows. Their off-stage lives were often high scandal, so adding to their popular appeal, distinguished exponents of what came to be called glamour; that was in contrast to the lives of their Hollywood successors who were subject to enforced secrecy.

Discretion was necessary when one of Offenbach's divas, Zoulmar Bouffar, used to visit him abroad, notably during summer seasons producing stage works at Bad Ems[10]. She was vivacious and gipsy-like, eventually suited to play the lead in *Carmen*. The letters to his wife listing daily routines at the health resort did not indicate that Bouffar and late-night gambling were on the menu. Yet in the French sense, he remained a 'good family man', and was too dedicated generally to misuse the casting couch. The interesting pre-war French film about him and Schneider[11] traces a romance between them, but that is nonsense; their volcanic rows were concerned with contracts and payments, but she could not hold out against his music.

La Diva (1869) was a romanticised version of Schneider's life, made into a sumptuous operetta. Despite the new songs written for her voice, it did not gain instant popularity, so the risk of mounting such an ambitious play-within-a-play restricted its performance at that time to Paris and Vienna. Now performed in Moscow under the title, *Prima Donna*, it includes in the personae the composer and Halévy, Schneider and three of her 'admirers', including Edward, Prince of Wales.

The Franco-German war of 1870 and the siege of Paris were to close entertainments, though this was the least of the humiliations following. The lighter musical theatre would be blamed by some for demoralising the nation. Offenbach's 'subversive' national origins made him a target for the chauvinist fringe, with their 'evidence' of his dangerous influences, such as ridiculing marriage in *Orpheus* and *Helen*; though the writers were not similarly blamed.

Henri Meilhac constructed excellent plots, and was the ideal partner for the lyricist, Ludovic Halévy, who was a sharp observer of Paris' life and inhabitants, the Boulevards, the financial frauds, the liasons between rich men and ambitious or needy girls. He and Offenbach stayed aloof from the corruption; they were the moralists, the realists who could convert the social scene into comic fantasies.

Halévy was busy elsewhere, but there was no immediate easing-up on political satire as Offenbach started working with a leading dramatist, Victorien Sardou. His *King Carrot (1872)* ridiculed in the main the republicans who gained power on the fall of Louis Napoleon III. The production put hundreds on stage, there were 32 scenes, with a gigantic presentation of the last days of Pompeii, of minimal relevance to the plot.

It was a shrewd response to the competition which was worrying the composer greatly. Charles Lecocq was composing more romantic operettas which could widen appeal down-market; at the other extreme, Hervé's zany musicals could be enjoyed by audiences who found satire too subtle. Offenbach would never fit into a stereotype or abandon the theatre of ideas. *King Carrot* was a challenging, idiosyncratic work which could appeal to high- and low-brow alike, and therefore is unthinkable in terms of commercial financing in our times[12].

Other works which followed quickly were musically of a high standard but were thought to lack Offenbach's characteristic flair. *The Pretty Perfumer (1873)* had the more serious theme of a young wife seduced, and its treatment came near to opera, enjoying success in London and Germany. *Madame Archduke (1874)*, with comic treatment of affairs between persons of differing rank, was a late Meilhac-Halévy work, but it lacked biting satire, because they were moving away from that approach.

There was a broad feeling that opera *bouffe* and its mockery were too political and losing fashionable appeal. Political insecurity induced the government to ban *The Grand Duchess* for some years after 1870.

One persistent abuse until the early 20th century at the major opera houses was the claque: people bribed to attend and applaud or deride individual singers. In *Bagatelle (1874)*, a work well described by its title, a young fan in a travesty role hands out rough justice to a tiresome claque in defence of the actress he admires. Duets for two sopranos and a snoring trio are the highlights.

Most commentaries make little of Offenbach's unique operetta written in English. In fact, *Dick Whittington* had the distinction of two enthusiastic reviews in a single edition of London's reputable theatre weekly, the *Era* (January 1875). A big impression was made by its *Barbaric Ballet* which was later performed in its own right. It was treated as if it represented African culture, so one critic did not complain that for once there were no swirling petticoats, delirium or headlong tumbling. Yet a slight rebuke was added; if the composer had condescended to visit London and the Bow bells, he could have added some local colour. Essentially a cosmopolitan, Offenbach preferred to invent his own.

Whittington was near enough pantomime, moving from lonely Highgate to a Mediterranean shipwreck and a riverside meeting with King Edward III. As many suspect, the hero became Lord Mayor through his 'never say die' spirit and the prodigious exploits of his cat.

For the next work, a suitable title in translation is *The Baker's Wife has the Dough*, in the spirit of its verbal humour. Operetta composer Renaldo Hahn valued its cabaret appeal, and in that style, he sang and recorded two insolent songs. One tells how a flour merchant's wife gets a checkered look through having two lovers, a coalman and her husband. *What price Virtue?* implies that such competition may increase marital ardour.

The Gaîté was the venue for an opulent show, *The Moon Voyage (1875–6)*. It was inspired by scientific optimism, and the theory that in one phase, the moon comes within jumping distance of earth. Much of the humour is derived from the eccentric attitude of the moon-dwellers to love and sex. A second Jules Verne conception was dramatised a year later; *Doctor Ox* also had extraordinary stage and sound effects for an elaborate joke about the release of laughing gas. Monsieur Verne was keen that such ideas should be given the most farcical treatment, and was not disappointed.

Spending on ambitious projects over a decade forced Offenbach to recoup money by foreign tours; Austria was artistically worth frequent visits because he could create new works or versions in the German language. The U.S. trip in 1876 would reduce creativity and was hardly necessary because he was already famous there. Audiences were hoping for a virtuoso of the cello as charismatic as Paganini or Liszt. Perhaps they had heard the observation of Paris diarists, the Goncourts: *a skeleton with pince-nez who looks as if he is raping a cello.*

He was terminally ill, and a victim of arthritis. Conducting as a celebrity was for him very tiring, though he was not above pulling a stunt. With Sunday concerts in Philadelphia restricted to religious works, he attempted without success to include love songs for *Helen* and *The Grand Duchess*, to liturgical texts in translation. Apart from the profits, a most positive aspect of that visit was the presence under his baton of John P. Sousa, Offenbach's American successor, later to write superlative marches and lively operettas.

In the final years, librettists Henri Chivot and Alfred Duru prepared two superior comic operas to inspired music. *Mme Favart (1878)* was the romanticised story of a famous 18th century comédienne subjected by an aristocrat to prolongued sexual harassment. In the middle- act finale, there is a piquant mock-dénouement in the Meyerbeer style, as a clownish police agent infatuated with the real 'culprit' is hoodwinked into making a false arrest.

In part, *Mme Favart* uses 18th century pastiche, and some of its ensembles are Mozartian. With an entirely credible plot and fine characterisation, it was performed successfully as a straight play in London years after its operatic triumph in the West End.

The Drum-major's Daughter (1879) was considered once a successor to Donizettis' popular opera *bouffe, The Daughter of the Regiment*, which had also been composed for Paris. There is no shortage of exhilaration, or French delicacy, this time with the exquisite *Tailor's* aria. In praise of Napoleon's Italian expeditions, emotive use is made of the great marching song of the 1789 Revolution, *Le Chant du départ* (Song of Farewell) by Méhul.

This was the last of the works which satisfied Offenbach mania in London by the 1870s, one of nine performed at the vast Alhambra, Leicester Square, between 1872 and 1880. In any one of those years, some half dozen might have been seen, lasting several weeks in the capital or going on tour.

Offenbach would often haul himself onto the stage to demonstrate a new routine or galvanise his flagging troupe during rehearsals. Aware that his old rival was dying, Hervé agreed to raise spirits and box office receipts by the novelty of singing under his baton in *Orpheus.*

Offenbach composed until the end, which came as he had barely completed the piano score of *The Tales of Hofmann* and left two operettas[13] unfinished. *Hofmann* has such an enigmatic plot that not many composers would have tackled it, a psychological drama studded with ironies and anti-climax. It demanded all Offenbach's acquired skills, and by adding a rich lyricism, he created a masterpiece in grand opera. Though it was his swan-song, many critics believe his most important achievements were among the operettas or operas *bouffes*, at least ten of about 40 full-length stage-works he created. Some 20 came in the '70s, and the best of them are still likely to be revived successfully with imaginative productions. The Offenbach cult will run into the 21st century, and unfamiliar works will once more receive critical acclaim.

5   *Suppé and Golden Vienna*

Milos Forman's filmed version of the play, *Amadeus*, recreated the carnival atmosphere of a popular Viennese theatre-cum-music hall presenting a lusty burlesque of *Don Giovanni*. A harlequinade, circus folk and animals were on stage, the audience joined in the singing, and there was spontaneous communication across the limelight. In the film, Mozart was present as a guest and thoroughly enjoyed it, but his wife Constanza found it vulgar. The producer, Emmanuel Schikaneder, had invited Mozart in the hopes of persuading him to collaborate in a German work for this theatre.

Mozart saw such ventures as a means to raise standards of popular taste. He was bitterly at odds with music's traditionalists at the court theatre, for whom Italian was sacrosanct. He approved Schikaneder's aims and methods for developing a style of people's opera, and earlier he had composed a few works for performance in German at theatres open to the general public. There was even support for this idea from the 'enlightened' Emperor Joseph II, but that ended with his death in 1790.

Schikaneder and Mozart worked on *The Magic Flute (1791)*, an idiosyncratic combination of music, comedy and pantomime, and a masterpiece now respected as 'high' opera; its populist features are not stressed today, though they create most of the laughter. With Mozart's death following soon after, that was an appalling loss, among other things, for the progress of music theatre.

Schikaneder went on to sink most of his money into ambitious plans, rebuilding in 1801 the Theater an der Wien, destined to play a distinguished role in Vienna's cultural history, performing great compositions by Beethoven and Schubert. Yet nothing comparable to the Mozart initiative followed, and Vienna's light musicals were not good enough to be housed there: the farce (*Posse*) and the comedy with songs (*Singspiel*) were the normal fare. It was some six decades before the theatre would open its doors to a new, sophisticated style of musical entertainment. It was markedly different from the Mozart-Schikaneder conception, though they would have approved. The impetus came with the arrival in Vienna of Offenbach's works in translation.

Franz von Suppé (1819–95) was born an Austrian citizen in Dalmatia and educated in Italian as a first language, but in his formative years, he would have become familiar with music of Austria to the north and of the Slav people of his home region. In his twenties, as a result of writing a talented opera, Suppé was invited to study with Donizetti whose bel canto style became an important influence in his own compositions, just as Wagner later inspired him, notably in orchestration.

By the 1840s, Suppé was providing music for the popular Viennese theatre, at first hack work for numerous shows which had no distinction. Yet he was also conducting Beethoven and other major symphonic works, and learned, like Rossini, to write exciting overtures, which he would then try to fit to a suitable musical. One such piece became an unwanted child which he sold for 8 thalers, a few pounds; some one hundred and fifty years later, it is still being performed throughout the world. *Poet and Peasant* will have earned a fortune for someone, a beautiful Suppé overture with a rousing conclusion. The reason for its special success must be one arresting theme, a model of the slow, long-flowing bel canto melody, in the manner of Bellini.

An excellent pastiche could be made from the best of his early stage music. *Alraunerl* is forgotten, but one hymn-like march was extracted, to become *O, my Austria*, the second national anthem.

In the 1850s, Suppé composed a parody on the style of the earlier Wagner, calling it *Tannenhäuser*, and a pastiche titled *Mozart*. This imitative ability was a particular gift, but not approved in all quarters, especially when applied to Vienna's favourite son, Franz Schubert (1864). Some disliked Schubert's intimate style being subjected to Suppé's startlingly modern orchestration. It was also argued that the slight plot which winds through Schubert's great song-cycle, *Die schöne Müllerin*, was unsuited for dramatisation, and that he should never be sensationalised as a boozing womaniser.

With the first of his works still often performed, *Das Pensionat*, (The Girls' Finishing School), 1860, Suppé reversed the frequent imbalance of male and female voices in opera. Twelve girl soloists proclaim their enthusiasms for the fine arts and a classical education, but relaxation brings gossip about Paris fashions, then trying-out a new craze, the bolero, a slow, sensuous dance.

Some conventional ballet music follows, but one girl complains that it is boring and proposes a 'proper dance'. This is a galop which affects them most improperly, with the more daring attempting the dangerous cancan. The girls are duly rebuked.

The heroine has an impoverished lover, a young man who is hovering just outside the institute; he will pretend to have 'fallen' for the head-mistress, compromise her and use blackmail to secure a job in the college.

This trifling plot was adequate for a one-acter, and had to sustain an impressive musical score of eight songs, including a richly scored finale for six soloists and double chorus, with a fine melodic sweep which recalls without plagiarism the great sextet from Donizetti's *Lucia di Lammermoor*.

There was a discrepancy in scale and quality between Suppé's musical talents and the slight farces he was obliged to work with. He was aware that any progress must depend on moving towards a fusion of words and music, such as in the new Paris operettas. A significant advance was *Ten Girls without a Man*. It is an ingenious farce involving the only operatic hero to have developed an obsessive infatuation for the back view of a girl whom he cannot otherwise identify.

A hazardous search brings him into a household where the father determines to couple him, if necessary by shot-gun wedding, to any one of his ten daughters. They are charming evidence of promiscuous travels around Europe's opera houses, nine singers having presented this Casanova with a child, and in one case twins. Since they have all inherited their mothers' gifts, they are trained to give every visiting male a staged entertainment based upon their respective national dresses and culture. Florid Italian singing and a restrained English ballad are among the enticing offerings, but the stranger is not swept over by any of the girls.

The father is convinced that their skills have been perfected under his régime of harsh discipline. Dressed as a military band, they play a sprightly march, and the drummer is the servant girl who possesses the face to match the back. There can be no objection to her being selected, as the young man has just been identified as the eleventh offspring carelessly mislaid for some two decades.

In 1865 Suppé adapted a superior playlet, *Beautiful Galatea*, with a story close to that for Massé's French opera and William Gilbert's play. It is based on the legend of the artist Pygmalion being ravished by the beauty of his statue. At his urging, Venus makes her human.

Galatea scintillates, and musically in a style which is thought to show Offenbach's influence, notably the waltz. Legendary names are domesticated; King Midas becomes an art dealer, and Ganymede, the cupbearer of the gods, is Pygmalion's lowly apprentice, which does not prevent Galatea taking a fancy to him. In Pygmalion's absence, he accepts a bribe to let Midas see her, and he tries to win her over with jewels. She is curious to be kissed, and selects as her partner Ganymede (a kissing duet). A drinking song praises 'classic' Greece, but does not produce real cameraderie to overcome male possessiveness, specially when Pygmalion returns. Galathea, though charmingly innocent, becomes drunk on wine, gets out of control and is once more turned into a statue by Venus.

Suppé's witty one-act score had unprecedented success in Vienna. Its plot has much comic potential, and many productions expand the dialogue to make a full evening's entertainment.

Light Cavalry, a military operetta for male voices, has such panache that the overture which is still so widely played is often mistaken for 'circus music'. It is one of those stage works struck down unjustly by an accident of history, appearing in 1866 just before the catastrophic defeat of the Austrian Empire by the Prussians at Sadowa. That hung over the nation for decades.

A story of outlaws who are not too wicked is always acceptable, from Auber's *Fra Diavolo*, (which Laurel and Hardy were to film), to Millöcker's *Gasparone* and Sullivan's *Pirates*. Suppé's *Bandits' Tricks (1867)* is an absurd frolic with lively music which made it very successful for some years.

Offenbach visited Vienna several times, where during his lifetime, more than 60 of his works were performed. He negotiated a lucrative long-term contract with the Theater an der Wien, despite the severe Austrian censorship. The satirical tones of the plays were noted, but as they were thought to be directed at the French and other foreign courts, local audiences were permitted to enjoy them.

Impresarios became keen to exploit the increasing demand for Parisian operettas with cheaper, home-made novelties. Suppé had the necessary skills, but he was strangely reluctant to create a larger work, probably because he was very busy and making sufficient money as a musical director.

The challenge was however taken-up by Johann Strauss, until then just a phenomenally popular composer of dance music. His first work, *Indigo and the 40 Thieves*, based on a well-known *Arabian Nights* fantasy, was good enough to justify a new career in operetta. This continued for over 30 years, though not often achieving the perfection of *Die Fledermaus (1874)*, an adaptation of a Meilac-Halévy work which Strauss may have seen in Paris. In the definitive version, two male leads are obliged to spend most of one action-crammed evening pretending to be someone else, and are brought to comic humiliation in the process. The remaining cast add to the fun of disguise throughout the fancy-dress ball of the second act.

Strauss rose magnificently to the opportunities this classic farce presented, and its success will have energised Suppé. In 1876 he was served with the first of two fine libretti by *Fledermaus* collaborators, Zell and Genée.

Fatinitza (1876) is one of the most inventive of all plays which have a rich element of burlesque and though funny throughout, its story is credible. The eponymous heroine (hero), Fatinitza, is a young Russian officer disguised as a woman in order to protect the girl he loves. He also enjoys dressing-up for its own sake, especially in the army stage shows. The girl-friend's uncle is his commanding officer, who develops an infatuation for Fatinitza.

The action takes place on the Turkish-Bulgarian frontier, so that the music exploits two styles in interesting contrast, Slavonic and near-Eastern. The scenario, originating from the French writer, Scribe, was adapted for the Turkish-

Russian hostilities which erupted in that region in 1876–7. Setting the Fatinitza role for a woman was appetising, and Suppé with this work reached a level of success to rival Johann Strauss.

The girl and her 'maid' are taken hostage as a result of a Turkish incursion, then find themselves abducted to a harem where the second act unfurls to suitably exotic music and a 'Turkish' shadow play is enacted. The blessing is that the Turks do not fancy Fatinitza, but the couple are, of course, rescued by Russian commandos from a pasha with lecherous intent.

The show has a distinguished septet, and three marches, one 'Bulgarian', one 'Russian' and a third which is intended to reassert military fervour over the power of love. Even so, it is in spirit more suited to a carnival, and the Viennese promptly stole it for themselves, adding fresh words:

Du bist verrückt, Mein Kind, du-u-u gehörst nach Wien (You're a wild one, you belong to Vienna.)

With its compelling rhythm, this march became an international 'hit', one of the first ever on such a scale, and the operetta reached European capitals and several New York theatres within a few years.

Suppé's next success was another Zell and Genée adaptation, not too faithfully, of anecdotes about certain youthful indescretions by Boccaccio whose classic tales often laugh at men being cuckolded; which explains why for this plot he appears in Florence incognito. He intends to seduce a girl despite her watchful guardian whilst his two companions discover opportunities for dalliance, even enduring a beating up to avoid compromising compliant women.

The play neatly overcomes the problem of dealing with episodes which could not be seen on stage, by using a narrator. One citizen is offered a seat at the top of a magic tree where he observes the men in varying stages of love-making, one with his own wife. A second victim is a cooper who carries on banging nails into barrels whilst his spouse enjoys herself with Boccaccio's friend. The male chorus of workers is accompanied by one of the most rumbustious rhythms in all opera, and eccentric even by Suppé's standards.

The music seems to come from both sides of the Alps, such as the serenades, *Mia bella Fiorentina* and the Germanic *Do I have your Love?* Tarantellas and marches abound and there is *Undici*, a stampeding chorus with a play on numbers especially appealing to the inebriated. The choral writing has the opulence of grand opera, and for its scope, verve and melodies, it rivals *Fatinitza* as Suppé's masterpiece.

Donna Juanita (1880) was an immediate success, as far as Paris and 100 performances in Barcelona, but the plot's similarity to *Fatinitza* told by comparison in the long run against it. This time, the British are the Peninsular War villains in occupied San Sebastian which a young French officer, René, enters disguised as Juanita. He smuggles his troops into the town which is duly captured, but not before having to resist sexual advances from not one but two older gentlemen.

Donna Juanita reflects the demands made by the most ambitious of Suppé's works. It was a worthy medium for Richard Strauss' great dramatic interpreter and soprano, Maria Jeritza, when she performed it in the 1930s at the New York Metropolitan Opera.

The Africa Journey (1883) follows a con man as far as Cairo, so giving Suppé further opportunity for exotic scene-painting. There was in 1887 an 18th century pastiche on the work of one of Europe's most important folk composers, the Swedish Bellman.

Today, the most direct points of reference are a large number of exceptionally tuneful and exciting overtures very widely recorded. Suppé's skill in orchestrating even won the admiration of Edward Elgar, himself an expert.

One critical verdict is that Suppé's seven stageworks from 1880 onwards did not enhance his reputation, and that from an enormous output, only a handful stand at the peak of his achievement. There is a similar judgment about Johann Strauss, and about the third of the great Viennese trio, Karl Millöcker (1842–99). At least two of his operettas are still often performed in German-speaking lands, *The Beggar-Student* and *Gasparone.*

They had established the definitive form and style of what came to be called the 'golden age' of classical Viennese operetta. A few contemporaries created single works which stand in the first rank, whilst hundreds of others were drawn to what became artistically and commercially most fashionable, like no music beforehand. Some of these were considered sensational at the time but not destined for posterity. That is of course also true of opera; both genres were hard task-masters. A broader view is that some thirty Viennese operettas are melodically in the top class, incomparably better than musicals in our times. With some of them, the main task would be to up-date the plots, and social values.

At the prestigious Viennese theatres, operetta required singers of top quality who could act and had charisma. It has remained a speciality for the city, and an outstanding attraction for Vienna's foreign visitors. It spread out and was imitated in other parts of Europe, with Berlin and Budapest in particular developing their own variants.

At the top level, it was the sister, not the poor relation of opera, over which it has one long-term advantage; the texts are more independent of music and can be revised to include matters of topical interest, and especially to cater for changes in humour, without harming the musical content. There should be gorgeous melodies and orchestration, like romantic opera; the main differences are that operettas depend more upon dance and recurring rhythms, and the music scores are less developed symphonically.

The finest works have well-constructed plots, and witty dialogue. In general, 'love' is not taken too seriously; it may be gallant, illicit or foolish. Men who are trying too hard become the objects of laughter, or worse. Generally, the romantic leads are soprano and tenor whilst the lower the vocal pitch, the less successful in love and the more comical the role.

By 1900, the leading composers had died or were inactive, but the Viennese style was to receive new impetus. For the years when musicals depended for success on their quality, not media hype, *The Merry Widow (1905)* was to become the greatest stage sensation ever experienced to that time.

Based on a Meilhac-Halévy play, it is witty and risqué, with marriage to be contracted in the interests of the state, whilst sex may be enjoyed in adultery and visits to Paris' night-clubs, especially by diplomats. *The Merry Widow* had the qualities to be an addition to the 'golden age' works, but the composer, Franz Lehár, promptly told London impresario, Gerge Edwardes, that he was not in the business of writing 'funny music'. A much-travelled Hungarian bandmaster, Lehár could write in many exciting, exotic styles, but his operettas became increasingly serious and passionate. Other young men rapidly arrived to establish this new fashion, more sentimental than the previous style. The 'silver age' of Viennese operetta had arrived, its primacy lasting until World War II.

The Beggar Student – Saxons and a 'fifth column'

6   A Comedy of National Pride

Librettists Zell and Genée worked with the main composers of the golden age of Viennese operetta, the last three decades of the 19th century. They offered an exceptional play, *The Beggar Student (1882)*, to Karl Millöcker (1842–99), at the time musical director of the Theater an der Wien. Like *Die Fledermaus*, it finds humour round every corner and it inspired Millöcker to compose a masterpiece.

Comedy rather than farce, it makes play with class distinction, national rivalries, and male-female adversity. The action is located during the wide-ranging Northern War in Crakow, the traditional Polish capital, in 1704, soon after the Saxon ruler Augustus had bribed his way into becoming the elected King of Poland. His German-speaking troops form the garrison and are on polite but guarded terms with the citizens. Their commander, Colonel Ollendorf, has whilst dancing risked kissing a Polish girl, Laura, on the shoulder. She has responded by slapping him firmly with her fan, an event which has preceded the action of the play but is referred to often by him and with more heat than one might expect from a seasoned military man in the public gaze. The musical phrase: *I just kissed her on the shoulder*, is one of the best remembered in all Viennese operetta.

The opening scene takes place in a jail presided over by a Saxon oaf, Enterich, who unsupervised from above runs a corrupt régime, often in an alcoholic haze. His peace disturbed, he is first heard barking at a gathering of Polish women, who are clamouring to see the prisoners, no doubt aware that only a bribe will work the trick. In his most officious manner, he confronts the female chorus, but taking stock of what they have brought the prisoners, he consents. With their music growing to a swell, he adds in an aside the words 'registration, then confiscation'.

The prison is the unexpected venue chosen by Ollendorf to meet his three senior officers; meeting them at the gate, Enterich adopts a fawning attitude, but they are distracted by

47

the pleasure of reliving the dance-floor humiliation of the previous evening. On arrival, Ollendorf seeks to enlist their sympathies, having already probed the matter too far for his own comfort. Through bribery, he has acquired a letter in which the girl's mother has ridiculed him as a prospective suitor and described the Saxons as fit only to live in stables. Only a Polish prince would suit for her daughters.

His frustration is given full rein in a distinguished aria of abruptly changing rhythms, pulsating but tender on speaking of Laura. In the furious galop which follows, he threatens to extract full revenge, not least for this insult to the whole Saxon army. He intends to find a presentable young Polish prisoner who will in return for a promise of freedom agree to impersonate an aristocrat, win Laura's heart and marry her on pretence.

Enterich says he has two such 'items' in charge; Symon is always looking for the easy way, and once selected, cannot refuse the offer. He and his young compatriot sing a fierce mazurka, not to the liking of their Saxon masters.

He is duly presented by Ollendorf at the elegant end of the Cracow Fair as Prince Wybicki, rich and keen to marry a local girl within a week. The supposition that any woman would fall for good looks and a title was specially plausible in 18th century Poland where an unusually oversubscribed nobility served no useful purpose other than to gratify vanities. Yet even in that milieu, Ollendorf is aware that Laura's mother is widely ridiculed for her snobbery:

> *We must protect our reputation and show disdain in all we do.*
> *For we're the backbone of the nation; though short of cash, our blood*
> *is true.*

So shopping is nothing but an occasion to be admired; she reminds her daughters that refined people need food for the mind, culture, whilst only the vulgar masses indulge their physical appetites. At the buffet, she orders meals of potatoes and water, which is why her younger daughter Bronislava has until now little interest except an appetite.

Symon boasts of his confidence with women, but with a song which places happiness close to sadness, there is a touch of Slavonic wistfulness. Even if he and Laura were not instantly attracted, her mother, Palmatica, overwhelmed by his status, would be rushing the girl into marriage. The Colonel's scheme will be undermined by genuine feeling between the young couple.

The wedding must be worthy of a rich aristocrat; this will cost him a fortune which he is forced to borrow. As the lovers start their flirtation duet, he joins in, at first encouraging the romance, Mephisto-like. Yet he soon begins to rue the additional expense whilst the other officers encourage him with the words 'revenge plan' in a vigorous ensemble. Symon, who claims to have seen many European beauties, praises Polish women in patriotic music.

A major achievement of Millöcker's composition was to highlight the widely perceived differences between Polish and Austro-German musical idioms. The mazurka is a distinguishing Polish rhythm, with its stress placed on each second note of three, in contrast to the waltz. The work's appeal is enhanced by these variations of triple time, and the Poles' songs are in turn vigorous, graceful and humorous, with two fine arias for the three lead women.

The first of these is the shopping trio, and the second in Laura's dressing room, summons 18th century elegance in musical style to restrain the girls' romantic enthusiasm.

The back-slapping Saxons express themselves in confident, four-square music, but occasionally with a suggestion of laughing up their wide sleeves at the chance Ollendorf might suffer a second defeat. The phrase which introduces Wybicki to Laura has a mocking touch, and it becomes a motif used to ironic effect on occasions.

Since a prince would be entitled to an aide, Symon's companion Jan has also been granted conditional freedom, and as he rapidly enters into a romance with Bronislava, there are duets which rise to ecstatic moments. Jan had been imprisoned as a suspected member of the Polish resistance movement. This supports 'King Stanislaus', who in reality was the puppet of a rampaging Swedish army but for the purpose of this fiction, is to be seen as the virtuous pretender. The Saxons, in their red-yellow uniforms and three-cornered hats, are riding for a fall, but are not really villains.

Symon even bungles a last-minute attempt to inform Laura of his real status, but convinced from interchanges during their second duet that she could love a pauper, proceeds as

arranged. The marriage ceremony occupies much of the
second act, an opulent occasion, climaxed by another exhilarating mazurka, one of the finest in the classic repertoire. It is
danced by the hired corps de ballet, but with festivities at a
peak, the ceremony is interrupted by Ollendorf's staged party
coup; all the male prisoners have been briefly released to burst
in and 'celebrate' the marriage of a Polish beggar to a fine
lady. At the head of a bedraggled file marches Enterich to
flute and drum accompaniment and an appallingly vulgar
street chorus. He is Ollendorf's choice to deliver in his
grotesque person the final humiliation to this most distinguished gathering. They are reduced to silence as he holds
stage, mocking the 'success of the beggar student', a title
once contemptuously thrown at him by the Colonel. Act II
ends with a powerful choral finale of conflicting emotions,
Ollendorf's sense of triumph to the fore:

> *Once he kissed her on the shoulder, just a mere escapade,*
> *But she nearly knocked him over, now his debts are repaid.*

before Symon, distraught, faces the Poles' fury and is evicted
from the wedding.

Jan now reveals his identity, so that he can prevail on his
impoverished friend to serve his political cause; to surrender
under the guise of being a higher-ranking leader whom
Ollendorf must capture in the hopes of neutralising Stanislaus' support in the city. This enables Jan to hand Symon
over in return for a large sum of money from the Saxons, then
uses it to subvert the Polish forces guarding the citadel. As a
result, the city falls to an insurgent army and the Saxons are
forced to surrender. Symon will receive at least one of the
bountiful titles from the new King and both Laura and
Bronislava are happy to accept him into their family.

Despite all, Ollendorf exits as a gallant loser, having won
some sympathy in his aria detailing how, being in turn commandant and diplomat, in middle age he cannot compete
with young men for women's affections; so life is not all about
status and privilege.

He is thoroughly memorable, an outsize *buffo* character, his
bombastic manner set-off against the pretentiousness of Palmatica, so apparent in the rounded phrasing of her music.
The other Poles get their share of invigorating galops, one of

which in the original German version refers to their fancy for drinking champagne from girls' shoes.

This is an opera of rich contrasts, in culture, posture and decorative colour. In 1884, its potential was seized upon in London for an enlarged four-act production at the Alhambra. The plot has been spiced with a farcical element in the 1995 production at Berlin's Metropol theatre. By adding two more characters and comic intrigue to the traditional plot, it extends the drama without impairing its musical features. As a bonus, instead of being narrated, the incident of the kiss is played-out in a colourful ballroom scene at the start.

A second additional scene follows, in a Polish tavern where a young Saxon officer is enjoying a meal in a convivial atmosphere. Bearing the ludicrous title, Lieutenant von und zu Pillnitz, when he lets slip that he is unknown to the garrison unit which he is about to join, he is promptly seized by the attendant 'freedom fighters'. They decide to replace him with a spy and the choice falls upon the innkeeper's daughter, Maria, so that a soubrette role is neatly integrated into the ensemble writing.

She is the first officer to arrive for the rendez-vous at the prison and tells Enterich of the Commandant's impending visit. He gets into a panic that Ollendorf will discover the prisoners have been let out of their cells, and other irregularities. The jailors rush to fill the cells once more, whilst Enterich is further unhinged by Maria's nervous strutting. This slender figure then continues her charade, trying to impress Ollendorf with military precision. Such a preposterous marionette show would raise his suspicions if he were not preoccupied with the Laura problem, but once accepted, Maria takes her place as an effective clandestine contact with Symon and Jan.

The stage directions specify that Enterich should be lame, and at the Metropol, he is transformed into a gnome-like figure with a wooden leg, seen at his funniest when barking orders in an uncouth Saxon accent to keep in step a freakish procession of drop-outs led onto the wedding concourse.

Into our own times, German and Austrian audiences continue to laugh at these Saxons and their accents. The work's performances were only stopped briefly on the orders of Hitler during the years following the invasion of Poland in

1939. It has been filmed in German five times, so that the earlier 1931 version with the dynamic Jarmila Novotna is of special historic interest. Some of the songs are widely known, but outside German-speaking lands, the work is under-performed. In recent years there have been at least two productions in London, and it is often in the Warsaw repertoire.

7   The Gaiety Theatre

Low quality entertainment had been the norm at the London theatres for as long as anyone could remember in the 1860s. Drama had reached its depths ; in 1870, *The Times* critic congratulated Irish-born Dion Boucicault on being the only contemporary dramatist who understood the need for sophisticated characterisation, and well-constructed, suspenseful plots. His plays stand out among those that could have an occasional revival in our own times.

Provision of large-scale music-making around 1850 was inadequate for a great capital. There were no well-established concert halls, opera seasons were haphazard and financially risky, Italian being the accepted language. With the lack of encouragement for the native product, it was remarkable that two prolific composers had emerged, Richard Balfe and William Wallace. Both Irish-born, their fine melodies ensured they were performed abroad, and in countries where opera was much better established.

One boy who wandered in curiosity around London's streets during the '40s was a journalist in the making, and his imagination extended far beyond the drab scenes he saw. When he peeped into deserted theatres, he imagined what might have been, visions which were to motivate him during his mature life.

Born in 1827 to poverty, John Hollingshead worked hard to educate himself, wrote for a journal on social reform, then still a young man, became the drama critic of a quality newspaper. He wanted to fight the restrictive legislation, similar to what had held back Paris' theatres. An early venture was to introduce the cancan to London's Lyceum theatre through a famous Parisian dancer. He avoided prosecution by ensuring that the men would not see what they specially wanted, a bare female leg ; tights had become a convention and a safety measure in burlesque.

By the age of 40, he was pushing for spectacular productions at Leicester Square's Alhambra, but that theatre would rapidly develop into London's largest centre for Continental musicals without his services, because he soon left to become his own boss.

He was open to original ideas, and his determination and organising ability persuaded others to lend him the money he lacked. In 1868, he became the impresario of the Gaiety, a renovated theatre in Catherine Street opposite the Aldwych, fairly large in the ornate 'classical' style imitated from Paris; it was assumed to be a financial liability which would ruin him within a year. Consumer-friendly, he improved the comfort of the audience, providing alcohol and restaurant facilities – especially desirable because of the length of the shows – and he cut out overcharging for amenities, whilst distributing free programmes and making them more readable. He began to make visits to the Continent, studying the latest in entertainment, bringing back artistes and eventually theatre troupes.

One new policy would be unthinkable today: maximum flexibility, no tickets to be booked more than two weeks in advance, so that schedules could be altered for important promotions. Since there were three stage events every evening, this gave scope for innovation; two of the items would be selected from short plays, farces, ballets and romantic operettas.

Many of his selections sound impressive nearly a century and a half later; obscure Restoration drama, Richard Sheridan, Boucicault, adaptations of classic English and Continental literature. Shakespeare was to be played unexpurgated, and there was a Falstaff version with additional clowning and a musical score by Arthur Sullivan.

The third part of each programme would keep alive what Hollingshead called 'the sacred lamp of burlesque', and in so doing create a fantasy world which had its origins in those childhood imaginings. In London, there was no shortage of third- rate burlesque – trivial, cliché-ridden and crammed with weak jokes, and a tradition of extravaganzas. These were short, farcical versions of familiar stories, with unsophisticated humour that never reached to satire, and supported by popular melodies.

For some 20 years Hollingshead would supervise the development of burlesque to much higher standards with a stable house production team. That included Meyer Lutz, musical arranger and composer of several theatre 'hits', with Nellie Farren filling the central role as travesty comédienne acting-out famous names from history and legend.

Young William Gilbert gave the Gaiety a good start with a new burlesque of Meyerbeer's grand opera. *Robert le Diable*, a man prone to wicked deeds unless the fair sex could bring him under control. All English burlesques were given comic sub-titles, and *The Nun, the Dun and the Son of a Gun* set the tone. For Robert's famous ordeal with naughty nuns, the audience thought Tussaud's Chamber of Horrors had been brought to life. Even so, waxen ladies were a safe option compared with a trendy 1990s' production of the genuine *Robert* in which defrocked nuns would be unfrocked nymphomaniacs.

Gilbert might laugh at sex, but once he produced his own works, he'd never place it on stage. It became his intention to clean-up the theatre scene with 'respectable' family entertainment suitable for grandma and the children to see. So he broke with the Gaiety company and others, even banishing from his shows the fashion of girls wearing tights.

Less inhibited fare was plentiful, such as Hervé's burlesque-pantomime, *Aladdin II*, prepared to an English text by Alfred Thompson and introduced at the Gaiety for Christmas 1870. In his memories, Hollingshead wrote of his childlike pleasure over the wit and antics of this ultra-spectacular. He was enthralled with the 'dancing of two extraordinary men who fall into one hole to be shot up through another', and a scene of the villainous magician being turned by the genie of the lantern into a mechanical jack-in-the-box with breath-taking leaps.

Thompson was no Gilbert, but he cut down on relentless punning, substituting the occasional literary misquote: *A thing of beauty is a toy forever,* and writing lyrics with a mildly satirical edge:

> *Between you and me, I'm a grand Taicoon,*
> *I've millions under my thumb*
> *For many there be beneath the moon*
> *Who to cares like mine succomb.*
> *For fleets and for armies I tax the land*

Though my enemies insist,
My standing troops on paper stand,
And my navies don't exist.

Thompson was one of the breed of theatre executives who create immense successes, then are forgotten whilst posterity recalls composers and impresarios. His ballets had rave notices, and Aladdin II initiated a pre-Mikado cult for things Japanese.

He wrote most of the Gaiety's early burlesques, from *Columbus* to *Wat Tyler M. P.* ; the assertion that the music for such works was by the 'best composers available' was very modest considering it was taken, or stolen, from the greatest of recently deceased Italian and living French composers. Paris 'culture' was for a time to be in the forefront; Hollingshead jumped at a colourful new work by Offenbach, *The Princess of Trebizond*, in a softer tone and very tuneful, and lured him into a rare London visit. Whilst there, he gave permission for a curious concoction; though he was no African explorer, his impressions of that continent, real or imagined, were briefly among London fashions. For April 1871, the theatre were pleased to announce *Malala, an African extravaganza*, based on his music.

Within a few years, the number of Offenbach's compositions seen at the Gaiety reached double figures, including most of his world-famous spectaculars. There was an extended season of French opera, including two long-term favourites, Auber's rollicking *Fra Diavolo* and Hérold's ghost story, *Zampa*, but when a brave attempt to encourage new operas by English composers faltered, there were critics to be faced.

Alongside the Alhambra, the most topical developments in opera *bouffes* and comic musicals were to be found at the Gaiety, and with certain works likely to be revived again in the 21st century such as Suppé's *Beautiful Galatea* and Charles Lecocq's *Daughter of Mme Angot*.

The Gaiety also saw what is now an historical curiosity, *Thespis*, the first collaboration of Gilbert and Sullivan concerning the gods coming to earth in a bid to revive their youth. This was judged a failure, partly because the Gaiety company was not ideally suited for Sullivan's 'classic' operatic idiom. The work can no longer be reassessed, much of the score being lost.

By 1873, in the first five years, at least a dozen composers still admired today had light or farcical stage works performed there in authentic versions. For several burlesques, music was prepared by Lutz, especially for the highlight of the *pas de quatre* performed by the four comic leads. There was a *Don Juan* entertainment, called *Don Giovanni* to indicate that Mozart's opera was being sent-up, with the Don's wily servant Leporello played by a woman. Victor Hugo's feverish play, *Ruy Blas*, was given the subtitle, *The blasé roué*. Copyright laws hardly operated, but the most recent compositions had some protection; *Faust-up-to-date* was not permitted to use any of the original music, nor was *Carmen-up-to-data*, for which Lutz' *pas de quatre* was to become the Gaiety's popular theme song.

Bringing classics 'up to date' was a main source of humour, executed with love and without condescension. Successful burlesque relied on sketchy rather than brilliant texts; a profusion of on-stage activities and rich improvisation were essential. The Gaiety shows would feature a quartet of fine comedians weaving their own routines into the action, and for many years hardly permitting success to break up their team. Some would introduce topical social, political and international news items. Flexibility enabled the troupe, or part of it, to tour the provinces whilst special visiting attractions were at the Gaiety, and in this way, a nation-wide reputation was achieved.

In the period to the turn of the century, leading London theatres progressed to their commercially most successful phase, and the Gaiety built a distinctive image and group loyalty. There was no need to call in additional 'stars' – people who often regardless of talent were able to increase box-office, increase the theatre takings but receiving a large share. Artistically, the London stage was in a far more healthy condition a century ago than the one we now know.

One problem in researching contemporaneous articles on stage productions and individual performances is that too many 'critics' wrote what amounted to 'puffs' for which money habitually changed hands. Hollingshead had no time for these manoeuvres, though at an early stage he instituted a house magazine to propagate the breadth of entertainment he was offering.

By 1886, ill health forced him to find a partner, and he chose the young manager of the Savoy theatre, George Edwardes, who rose to similar public esteem over 30 years. The cause of burlesque suffered blows around 1890 with the permanent indisposition of Miss Farren and the death of other popular favourites, whilst its first patron was no longer making the big decisions, By the early '90s, musical comedy was the novelty and Hollingshead spoke of its appeal in uncomplimentary terms:

> *It offers a clever concoction, having neither beginning, middle or end, and therefore admirably adapted for an after-dinner audience who want to hear a song or see a dance or stare at a particular young lady through double-barrelled opera glasses.*

To posterity, this comment is no longer controversial but we can infer something about his ideal in burlesque. Unlike musical comedy, its objectives were not restricted by 'popular' fare. Starting with nothing but a famous character or myth and a talented cast, it had to impose its own logic, wit and fantasy, a cohesive mixture of dialogue, mime, spectacle, music and humour.

Edwardes was no purist, seeing musical comedy as the big money-spinner of the following decades, with burlesque being gradually phased out. He gave the Gaiety Girls publicity far beyond what his predecessor had seen fit during his 18 years' rule.

Of the composers who came to prominence then, Sidney Jones had enormous success as far as many Continental countries with his *Geisha*, which is scarcely performed today. Leslie Stuart, composer of the musical, *Floradora*, is probably the most interesting, with a very catchy use occasionally of syncopated melodies. The fame of musical comedies of the period has been brief, at best one or two generations, though some of their melodies are still revived for enthusiasts of the genre.

The Gaiety's public image became centred upon glamorous girls, parallel wih the rise of the Folies- Bergère in Paris. Edwardes had wider ambitions, acquiring in 1894 the recently-built Daly's theatre, which was more expensive to run, had a large orchestra and gradually took-over the staging of superior musicals and operettas, including the great ones such as *The Merry Widow*, which were to arrive from Vienna after 1900.

The old Gaiety theatre was demolished in 1903, to permit road widening, and was replaced in three months by the new Gaiety, located on the corner of the imposing Aldwych building where it enjoyed fame and success for three decades. Hollingshead attended the formal leave-taking but outlived his theatre by no more than a year.

8 *Sullivan and Parody*

The music of Weber, Mendelssohn, the Frenchmen Auber and Hérold and the Italians, Rossini, Bellini and Donizetti would have been very familiar in musical households during the childhood years of Arthur Sullivan. As a student, he learnt clarity of style and instrumentation from the French, and the lightness of orchestral touch such as one finds in their overtures. The German operas of Weber were immensely impressive, and outside opera, Mendelssohn was one of the most performed of all.

Sullivan's gift for parody induced him to pay his respects to all of them, often humorously, and to composers of earlier centuries, such as Handel and Purcell.

Opera in London around the 1850s was performed mostly in Italian, regardless of the composer's nationality, and its musical appeal could act as a screen for many inferior works. Its idiom, words and imagery were often subjected to cliché, characteristic of all popular forms of entertainment. It was becoming the target of popular burlesques.

Sullivan made many allusions to the best of Italian opera in his own work, and in songs and choruses inspired by the lyrics of his partner, Gilbert. Already, in *Trial by Jury (1875)*, the musical world was impressed by his skill composing an ensemble, which in structure and languorous melodic style recalled the first act finale in Bellini's popular *Sonnambula*.

In early romantic opera, plots were often absurdly influenced by magic, such as in Donizetti's *Elisir d'amore* (The Love Potion), and *The Sorcerer* takes things further, with several ill-assorted couples under a spell proposing marriage. It includes a scene which parodies the Wolf's Glen episode from Weber's *Freischütz*, the most frightening scene in all opera when it was written (1821).

Much of *The Pirates of Penzance* is all-out operatic burlesque. A bevy of English beauties fall into the hands of the pirates, their nervous chattering in tense rhythmic conflict with a slow, resolute male surge. When the girls have been verbally seduced, it takes a late counter-blast from the heroine to plunge the party into the depths of Verdian anguish. There is also a time for her voice to float on eloquent coloratura passages, and to flutter through an airy Gounodesque valse.[1]

These maidens, though so numerous, share one father who, with the authority of a Major-General, calls upon the local constabulary to apprehend the pirates. In the high-flown language of opera *seria*, the prosaic sergeant in place of 'riots' uses the French word 'emeutes' mincingly rhymed with 'boots'. This is no hero, and the men's spirits sink:

> *For when threatened with emeutes*
> *And your heart is in your boots,*
> *There is nothing brings it round*
> *Like the trumpet's martial sound,*
> *Tarantara, Tarantara, Tarantara*

The trumpets and drum roll get the police marching before a startling intervention. In those days, respectable Italian women were never militant, but in German legends, the most unseemly events could involve them. A female chorus joins in solidarity with the forces of the law, an uplifting Wagnerian soprano to the fore, hardly dignified by a solitary double-bass. Relentless singing puts off the moment of action and the enraged Major-General cannot silence the policemen. They eventually file off *With Catlike Tread*, a little anthem inspired by the gendarmes' creeping chorus in Offenbach's *Brigands*, and continuing with one of Sullivan's finest marches.

In *Iolanthe*, fairies are forced into action like Walkyries, deployed by their queen in a war with the House of Lords. Yet they remain gentle, which explains why *Iolanthe's* Overture and opening scene sound like the successful opera Mendelssohn never wrote.

Satire of the military is a major theme in *Patience*, and often surfaces elsewhere. Before working with Gilbert, Sullivan inserted a call to arms, a *rataplan*[2], along with a recognition scene, both preposterous, into *Cox & Box (1866)*, a slight domestic farce to a text by F C Burnand.

* * *

Ruddigore (1887) was a departure from the social satire that had enlivened the preceding works. It concentrated on burlesquing fashions in acting, language and characterisation, in Gothic novels and Victorian melodrama. It is the funniest operetta ever to ridicule so much doom and gloom; Offenbach could have competed in this style if the French had been as interested in horror stories as the English or Americans.

Its Overture plays the healthy spirits of village life against the sunken world of evil and black magic. The sinister aristocrats are suggested by a spooky motto theme, dispelled by an embracing cornet tune of the kind so popular with Victorians. A Germanic march is paired with a sprightly, Sullivanesque tune, then some love music, rounded-off with a vigorous horn-pipe for an amorous sailor.

The fishing village of Rederring, Cornwall, would be an uneventful place but for ghastly goings-on decreed long ago. The evil knight, Rupert Murgatroyd, now deceased, once tortured a witch who before dying had pronounced a curse, that each of his heirs would die on the day he fails to perpetrate a wicked deed. Aunt Hannah explains, sounding like the witch in *Trovatore* telling of even more horrid events[3].

Hope is even fading for the under-employed bridesmaids subsidised by the community, whilst a most desirable maiden, Rose Maybud, despairs of the eligible but shy Robin. A cheery event is the unexpected arrival of his foster-brother, Dick Dauntless, the reckless man from the sea, the more significant because Gilbertian plots thrive on obscure family relations.

The bridesmaids are dallying with young strangers, 'bucks and blades' who 'with flattery sated', have left the town to sing pastorales, and enjoy other rural pleasures:

> *From charms intramural*
> *To prettiness rural*
> *The sudden transition*
> *Is simply Elysian,*
> *So come, Amaryllis,*
> *Come, Chloe and Phyllis,*

The music briefly suggests Bohemian dancing, and a familiar rhythm from Smetana's *Bartered Bride (1866)*, but overlaid with the solemn phrasing of English oratorio to reflect the girls' collective virtue. But no country idyll must delay; this is high drama, and Beethovenian chords introduce Sir Despard

Murgatroyd, the witch's living victim. His slow catalogue of grief is pitched in the deepest tones of the graveyard, charmingly mocked by his listeners. A century later, when popular culture admires the male voice wallowing in addiction and self-pity, this dialogue's symmetrical phrasing has a sharpened satirical edge:

> SIR D: *I once was a nice-looking youth, But like stone from a strong catapult I rushed at my terrible cult –*
> GIRLS: *That's vice.*
> SIR D: *Observe the unpleasant result.*
> GIRLS: *Not nice.*
> SIR D: *You are very nice looking indeed.*
> *Oh, innocents, just listen in time*
> GIRLS: *We do,*
> SIR D: *Avoid an existence of crime –*
> GIRLS: *Just so –*
> SIR D: *Or you'll be as ugly as I'm –*
> GIRLS: *No! No!*

To be loathed by these beauties, forced to infamous deeds but with the heart of innocence: he has the power to summon up the classical furies, but as a gentle villain, he has chosen these genial young bucks as the instrument of his will. The poetic explanation of their presence in the village suddenly rings false.

Yet his suffering is about to end. A close family secret discloses that Robin had once fled the curse, being Despard's older brother and the legal heir; the curse will now be directed at him, so he will lose his bride just after he's found the courage to propose.

What more tragic in comic opera than a betrothal undone? The bridal chorus has already been selected, so must not be wasted; *When the Buds are blossoming* is a madrigal with double chorus much in the spirit of the 16th century and Thomas Morley's *Now is the Month of Maying*.

Everyone knows Margaret was driven insane when Despard abandoned her on succeeding to the title, and she luxuriates in the condition. Her mad song does not ascend in an ecstacy of derangement, Italian style, and after a flute obbligato, there are no high coloratura notes; like Ophelia, English heroines should lapse into a mood of resignation, preferably on a bed of flowery imagery.

Relief is not far off; she will learn Sir Despard is free and willing to marry her. Dick proposes to Rose and in a finale of conflicting emotions, the assemblage are swept into an archaic dance of exceptional rhythmic verve.

Margaret and Despard start their new lives as models of Victorian respectability. She becomes a 'district visitor', but occasionally lapses into insanity, not surprisingly to a modern audience, considering the plight of many social workers. In *Ruddigore's* most eccentric dance, she and Sir Despard circle in sedate movements, both draped in the tight-fitting black clothes of Victorian primness and repression. Played dead-pan, it is a very funny scene set up by Gilbert's verses. One simple word perfectly fits the voyeurs in our own media-dominated age:

> MARGARET: *I was once an exceedingly odd young lady –*
> DESPARD: *Suffering much from spleen and vapours.*
> M.: *Clergymen thought my conduct shady –*
> D.: *She didn't spend much on linen drapers.*
> M.: *It certainly entertained the gapers.*
> D.: *My ways were strange, beyond all range – Paragraphs got into all the papers.*

For his new role, Robin (now Sir Ruthven) has developed a most sinister laugh. In the inflated rhetoric of 19th century drama, he apostrophises the forces of evil:

> *Away, Remorse! Compunction, hence!*
> *Come, guiltiness of deadliest hue!*
> *Come, desperate deeds of derring do!*

His determination lapses when a Union Jack is waved in his face. By the time the chorus pleads *Grant thou her prayer*, oratorio is ennobling all, with a Brahmsian phrase in the wood-wind, as Rose and Dick are betrothed.

Robin's new duties take him to the portrait gallery at Ruddigore Castle, where to a funeral march, eight previous Murgatroyd baronets descend from their picture frames, a gripping vision of spectral doom, to ghoulish music. Like operatic witches, they hurl a measured pile of insults at Robin, a *Miserere* of rising chromatic melody[4]. Other romantic allusions include a broad 'religious' theme in the manner of Gounod, horn calls, muted drum-beats, and the four-stroke 'fate' rhythm associated with the opening of Beethoven's 5th Symphony. Tension is relieved in a half-mocking chorus and Robin's sinking into bathos with 'Alas, poor ghost', which critics have always assumed relates to the *Hamlet* graveyard scene.

The recently deceased Sir Roderic conjures up the ghost world:

> *When the night wind howls in the chimney cowls, and the bat in the moon light flies,*
> *When the footpads quail at the night bird's wail, and black dogs bay at the moon,*
> *This is the spectre's holiday – then is the ghost's high noon.*

But a ghost's life is not all gloom and there are suggestions of secret revelries. They are urbane enough to advise Robin on legal niceties and falsifying income tax returns.

Robin needs to prove his suitability for dastardly crimes, particularly over women, and at least one abduction is necessary. His valet is sent to steal at random a maiden from the village, but he is careless enough to return with Aunt Hannah. She goes overboard in defence of her honour, provoking a knife-throwing fracas which in a modern court would turn assailant into victim. Sir Roderic once more vacates his picture frame and embraces her. This meeting of two former lovers was said to be too much for some English sensibilities, though it is balanced by a thoroughly edifying conclusion.

Robin sees his new life as fraudulent, so why not call the witch's bluff? He will shrug-off the curse . . . . . . if he has to die now, it really doesn't matter. This phrase sustains a complex, triple patter song in perpetual motion.

Ruddigore's première was followed by almost a year of nightly performances, highly successful by normal standards but not those of the Savoy operas; it was destined to be considered a work apart. The verve of the first act is not sustained throughout, and the plot wanders in the second, though many of the later numbers are outstanding, with some of Sullivan's finest descriptive and instrumental writing.

Its form and contents make it difficult material for the local amateur societies which help maintain the familiarity of most of the Savoy operas to the present day. It is unusually operatic and the three characters with split personalities require rare acting skills and a vocal range.

Some parts of *Ruddigore* are as joyful and exuberant as the best in Sullivan, and in a subtle score, the burlesque elements could not be excelled.

Donnerwetter – a Prussian officer breaks down

9 *Berlin Follies*

The first casualty of war is truth, someone long ago observed, and mainly as a result of two world wars, we were encouraged to think of the Germans as humourless. For Berlin, journalistic clichés might provide one-sided images, such as the 'centre of German militarism' and more recently, Europe's 'flashpoint' in the cold war.

Another perspective is of Berlin as a city of enlightenment, and in the past century with a deserved recognition for its theatres and cultural life. It had been a village during the 30 Years' War (1618–48) when foreign armies trampled at will across Germany, causing the deaths from sword, fire and famine of perhaps one third of her population. For this reason, an efficient standing army became a necessity for the cities especially of the north German plains unprotected by nature. The state of Prussia fulfilled this need effectively, but acquiring a reputation for successful war-mongering. Yet there were other important long-term features, such as a policy of religious tolerance which brought exceptional numbers of immigrants, Jews and French Huguenots, to become respected Berlin citizens.

The expanding city which was destined as capital of Prussia received waves of Germans seeking work, an underclass with little respect for privilege and status, expressing themselves in a local dialect which was as lively and cheeky as Cockney. Their entertainments, cabarets and songs often poked fun at the institutions of the state and the army. When Marlene Dietrich returned to her home town after thirty years of self-imposed exile, the song which received the warmest welcome asserted that no disaster would ever deprive Berliners of fun:

Wenn die tollsten Dinge in der Welt passiern,
Der Berliner wird nie den Humor verliern.
(No matter what madness affects the world, Berliners will keep their sense of humour).

Hitler was aware of the City's spirit and hated it; he intended to raze it to the ground, even more systematically than allied aircraft actually did during the last war, and replace its name with his own capital, Germania.

Berlin's theatreland would have disappeared, whereas sufficient of it remained in 1945 for partial reconstruction, so that we can sense something of its distinguished past and the buildings in one central area. Since the city is not yet widely billed as a holiday venue, most foreigners are unaware that it has exceptional attractions; its theatres gained from the fact that for 40 years Berlin was the largest town of two separated states, and the capital of one of them.

The traditional entertainment centre fell in the eastern part of the town centre, and the Soviet commandant on taking over called for opera to be reopened just four months after hostilities ended – in the only theatre standing, the present Metropol, home of operettas and revues. That is in the Friedrichstrasse which for over a century has been famous for its large theatres and small cabarets, its musical comedies, revues, dancing girls, comics and popular songs.

Because of the wartime devastation, photographs of old Berlin have a special poignancy, especially those symbolising a time of relative innocence at the turn of the century when most Germans saw their army in defensive terms, and when their culture was making its wider impact. That was an age of uniforms, long dresses, ostentatious hats, flowing moustaches, horse trams, barrel-organs, and quaint motor vehicles.

There were important theatres where the army was burlesqued by chorus girls in high-kicking boots, and several young composers would establish themselves in a new kind of musical, inspired by Berlin's traditions and giving back songs dedicated to the city's favourite localities, such as the Unter den Linden. Outsiders, Austrians such as Leo Fall and Arnold Schoenberg, wrote cabaret songs, and a favoured son of Berlin was Paul Lincke whose melodies travelled far abroad and who had first created the city's characteristic operetta-burlesque.

He was born near the city's waterways in 1866, losing his father in infancy, but had the musical talent to overcome poverty. By 1890, he was being contracted to compose parodies of famous operas for immediate performance, and his early productive operetta years were at the Apollo theatre. He spent as musical director two years refining his skills at Paris' Folies-Bergère, which was already a model for the world of light entertainment.

Lincke's first collaborator had been Heinrich Bolten whose gift was to write fanciful lyrics relating gently to mankind's capacity for escapism and self-deception. He wrote extravaganzas concerning ordinary citizens attempting super-human feats and legendary heroes caught up in commonplace situations. He populated Berlin's river with water nymphs, sent two plumbers along canal ducts to Scharaffenland (the German fools' paradise), and dramatised Venus and her companion gods enjoying Berlin's night life, much in the spirit of *Orpheus in the Underworld*.

Operetta is often more influenced by real events than many would assume. Bolten was an enthusiastic balloonist long before he sent four of his stage characters by this method to the moon. The debonaire Lincke composed the two-act *Casanova* in 1913, years after he established his own reputation as what the Germans call not altogether flatteringly 'ein Casanova'.

Bolten's lyrics were politically innocent, but Lincke also worked with a radical writer, Julius Freund. Their best-known revue came in 1908, *Donnerwetter*, now remembered in another musical by a sketch where a guards officer, in splendid white uniform, is driving along a Berlin street in a gleaming 1900-style car. He is accompanied by an actress all in finery, less interested in him than in showing a trendy image. In front of the wondering locals, the car breaks down, emitting fumes and threatening to explode. The couple lose all dignity scampering away, but while a mechanic gets under the car, the officer struts around the cat-walk, singing to the goose-step that compulsive song, *Donnerwetter*, a polite expletive indicating much self-satisfaction. If Freund was presenting the officer corps as overpaid lay-abouts, it is not surprising that they were forbidden to attend the theatre where this revue was taking place. When the Crown Prince did so, he was subjected to house arrest.

This may explain the consequence of a request by Richard Strauss, Humperdinck and others, that Lincke be made court composer, a similar honour to what Johann Strauss had received in Vienna. The Kaiser's response was negative; he did not consider him 'respectable' enough, unlike the conformist Arthur Sullivan whose music he specially liked.

Lincke's melodies in general were exceptionally euphoric, reaching the height of popularity by the time of World War one, cheering trops on both sides of the front line which stretched out hideously across Europe. He could be sentimental in an appealing way, but most of his tunes were in turn declamatory, airy, street-wise, childlike, and well suited in musicals to push the action along. Some of his music was intrinsically funny, and when Charles Chaplin's classic film *The Cure* was reissued with a synchronised score, zany melodies from Lincke's *Frau Luna* were included.

Frau Luna had started off very modestly in 1899, just another Lincke-Bolten one-act operetta, but it was to strike a special chord with Berliners, reflecting their feelings, aspirations, and habits. The theme pervading the final complexities of the plot was the partnership's finest inspiration; the interplay and ironies of hope and resignation, the ideal and the commonplace, symbolised in the assumed allure of life among the moon-dwellers against the comic banalities of a Berlin street scene.

Lincke's musical style was part-'classical', part-Berlin. He composed few operettas after 1918, mainly because he did not have the feel for the new rhythms, especially those from the Americas. Yet he remained at his conductor's podium until the war drove him out of town; Berlin's once 'best-dressed citizen after the Crown Prince' died a penniless refugee in 1946.

His most important long-term project after 1930 was to convert *Frau Luna* by incorporating some of the funniest ideas and music from his other compositions. So it happens, that Prussian officer from *Donnerwetter* makes his bombastic mark on Berlin's working, that is, useful classes. Highlights from other Lincke reviews were to be included: the city's acknowledged marching song from *Berlin Air*, and from the classical operetta on Aristopanes' *Lysistrata*, the balletic *Glowworm* sequences, which Anna Pavlova took around the world.

The distinction of the basic conception is that certain of the characters first seen in a Berlin street have their alter egos on the moon. The expedition is led by an enthusiastic young engineer fired up by the feats of acronautic pioneers in Berlin of the 1890s, and much of the humour of the moon adventures is linked to his extreme naïvety. In contrast, his three colleagues are so unimaginative that they reduce their conversations with the moon-dwellers to banalities.

This imaginative and comic potential partly explains why a farce playing for no more than one hour has been gradually built-up by Lincke and his successors into a four-act spectacular, the definitive Berlin folk-opera. With each new version, the first challenge is how to find an innovative characterisation of the moon queen. Glamorous certainly, but a sex symbol, a dignified autocrat or a night club hostess? In west Germany she has inevitably appeared leading the Rhine Maidens, and in the south, as a maid of the mountains. In the 1911 London version, she was determined to seduce three shy travellers, English to a man.

Always in repertoire, the current Metropol production has continued over ten years and is good enough to greet the new century. It has adapted plot, scenes and dialogue to the many political changes; in its 1987 version, its fourth act becomes time travel, jumping nine decades to satirise the division of Germany and the cold war from an Eastern perspective.

The two middle acts on the moon are extravagant burlesque, with a Frau Luna who is *une femme fatale*, but not laid back. She is an enlightened despot, a philosopher queen, very strict within a feminist régime. Positive health care and the athletic life are compulsory for all; for the youth, no backsliding into decadent ways, no opiates, no permissiveness.

Frau Luna appears on high in a phallic space capsule, cloaked in a shower of primary colours, guarded by goosestepping girls. She is a Venus of coloratura as she descends to meet the visitors from earth. The second lunar scene begins with a parody of the grand march from *Tannhäuser*, for the ceremonial entry of courtiers, soldiers, and government ministers. All posts except the menial ones appear to be taken by women. With dancing chorus supplementing the corps de ballet, the cat-walk seems excitingly overloaded at the climaxes. The lunar men seem effete and are submissive to this show of female strength.

Frau Luna has taken a fancy to the young astronaut, and

like the knight, Tannhäuser, he is expected to surrender. She propels him into a glowing water-bed, reminding him that he must do Berlin proud, but this makes him think of his fiancée and, unlike Tannhäuser, he resists temptation. Reluctantly she agrees to marry a persistent suitor in the shape of a stellar prince who looks like the *Donnerwetter* officer. He obligingly takes the Berliners home in his space ship.

Many versions have taken the Wagner burlesque beyond the music; analogies with the innocent Parsifal in a magic garden, a Siegfried-Brunnhilde send-up, Valhalla, the Venusberg, the Holy Grail.

Lincke's following operettas included *The Land of Indra, Fräulein Loreley*, and *Nakiri's Wedding*, all within a few years. In structure, they tend to follow the *Luna* pattern, with the operatic and other musical styles available for 'heroes' and clowns, licentious, privileged or duty-bound females; an exotic beauty (operatic soprano) desires a young Berliner on tour (light tenor), whilst his sweetheart (soubrette) waits faithfully at home, and a grand prince or army officer (baritone) is put through the hoops before the glamorous lady agrees to marry him, *faute de mieux*.

Of the later Berlin operetta composers, the most distinguished and versatile was Eduard Künnecke (1883–1953), from opera to cabaret songs and superior dance music with attractive 1920s rhythms[1]. Active in Berlin for most of his adult life, he favoured exotic themes for his music, and his leading characters spend much time dreaming.

His songs sometimes looked towards Viennese romance and Parisian wit, his more tongue-in cheek style admirably suited for the absurd tale of *The Cousin from Nowhere (1921)*, his great international success. Not following the recent Berlin tradition, it was effective with minimal resources, seven singers, but no chorus or ballet. This is a romance of hidden identities, sensuous melodies such as *Shimmering Moon* and the *Batavia Song*, and best played as a whimsical period piece. The early scenes are mainly concerned with a stranger who calls himself a wandering vagabond, giving rise to a song which achieved exceptional popularity abroad, and for millions who had never heard of the show.

In total contrast to this escapist entertainment, and partly a reaction against it, was *The Threepenny Opera*, a provocative essay in black humour based upon the story of *The Beggars' Opera* (London, 1728). That had burlesqued the conventions of Italian opera, especially as purveyed by G.F. Handel.

Brecht's play surfaced exactly 200 years later, using the original underworld characters to strike at venality and other human weaknesses within a corrupt business world. His collaborator was Kurt Weill (1900–50), a young Berliner who had composed symphonic and experimental stage works. *Happy End (1929)* offered a parallel challenge in human values, almost a companion piece. It brings the Salvation army into whimsical contact with the underworld, and the story has some affinity with that of the later American musical, *Guys and Dolls.* For the Brecht-Weill partnership, the most complex project was *The Rise and Fall of the City of Mahagonny*, as a *Singspiel* then as a large-scale opera. This contains a song which goes nowhere and whose lyrics could be the definitive anthem for the world's addicts:

> *Please show us the way to the next whisky bar,*
> *For if we don't find the next whisky bar,*
> *I tell you we must die, I tell you we must die.*

In lighter musicals, Berlin in the later 1920s was moving away from the fantasy-burlesques of the Lincke tradition, with more cosmopolitan productions reflecting the city's greater prominence in international operetta. Ralph Benatzky produced a Johann Strauss pastiche, *Casanova (1928)*, remembered for the *Nuns' Chorus*, and *White Horse Inn (1930)*, the most successful operetta compiled by the combined efforts of an unspecified number of composers. A sentimental work, humour was not too prominent in its making.

Theo Mackeben, who had influenced Weill's arrangement for small band in *The Threepenny Opera*, successfully up-dated Millöcker's *Countess Dubarry (1882)*, a story of King Louis XVI's mistress not being quite faithful. Its 1932 title was *The Dubarry*, perhaps more suitable because she lost her title as well as her head in the French Revolution.

The Blue Angel (1928), being a film which brought Marlene Dietrich to the fore, is more widely remembered both sides of the Atlantic as characterising pre-Nazi Berlin; but it is also a musical of quality. It has two fine songs, *Lola*, in come- and-get- me style, and *From Head to Toe, I'm made for Love*, which is better known euphemistically as *Falling in Love again*. It tells how an ageing professor abandons his career for an alluring actress, following her on tours, forced to play the Clown on-stage, and being driven to ultimate humiliation. Only its lack of the escapist spirit has detracted from deserved popularity as a stage show.[2]

The Jewish Weill and the socialist Brecht fled Germany within days of the Nazi take-over along with Friedrich Hollaender, who had composed the music for *The Blue Angel*, and had collaborated with anti-Nazi satirists in the preceding years.

The Nazis attempted to maintain the prestige of Berlin's theatres, but their racial and other policies drove out creative talent, and their ideology did not tolerate pointed satire, so that much deteriorated after 1933. In suppressing subversive ideas, they favoured escapist films and theatre; the musicals of the later 1930s were mainly reviews, dance and spectacle, not far from popular music which in distinctively German style could be of quality.

Probably the best Berlin revue-operetta of the Nazi period is *Masquerade in Blue*, by Austrian Fred Raymond (1900–54), who remains known for a song, *I lost my heart in Heidelberg*. He was composing for the Metropol theatre at the time (1937) and for *Masquerade in Blue*, there was a witty mock-csardas, *Juliska from Budapest*. The work has looked and sounded excellent in 1990s' Berlin, exploiting Latin American rhythms; with an imaginative production, this very colourful work can give the word escapism a good name.

The ambience, music and dancing of 1920s Berlin inspired the American musical, *Cabaret*, with music by John Kander. Since the 1970s, a greatly admired film version, with an altered plot, has been seen by countless millions, in English-speaking countries, so presenting a narrow but lively image of Berlin night-life.

Berlin's song-and-dance spectaculars may be seen daily, except Mondays, in at least three permanent theatres, so that it is one of the world's most active city for this range of first-class entertainment.

The Theater am Westen is a specially elegant building in the west part of the city, which housed the Berlin Opera for years after it was rebuilt. It now presents for short-term runs a sequence of musicals which in the best sense present to discriminating younger audiences works which delighted their grand-parents, such as *Grand Hotel, White Horse Inn, The Blue Angel* and even a glamorised *Threepenny Opera.* In 1996, there was a fine German-language version of *The Pirates of Penzance,* startling in parts as a full-blooded parody of Verdi's *Trovatore.* Proof that G & S can still be successfully translated, it astonished many Berliners and was retained for a second run.

The Metropol company celebrates its centenary in 1998 and shares with Vienna's Volksoper the reputation of the world's leading operetta-and-musical theatre with productions of international standard. Its repertoire and complement are extraordinarily large, and in any one week, up to six works might be seen. It features an incomparable range of satirical and romantic musicals, from *Orpheus in the Underworld* to Cole Porter's *Ninotchka,* imaginative and spectacular, but not at the expense of authenticity. Curiosities have included a German version of Wilde's *Importance of being Earnest* and *The Wizard of Oz.*

The Friedrichstadtpalast once acquired a reputation for opera burlesque, and was for a time associated with the great producer, Max Reinhardt. A new theatre had to be built by the 1980s, and now offers a succession of revues, with a speciality in its chorus girls and dancing. The style has deteriorated into a stereotyped cosmopolitanism, conceptually weak, form taking over entirely from content, so that, as Prinz Orlovski says in *Die Fledermaus,* 'once you've seen one, you've seen them all'; but that can be to the satisfaction of its regular clientèle.

One revue, *Four Cities,* opted for clichés as symbols: the familiar red coach of Berlin's overhead rail, a wedding cake and a waltz for Vienna, a cafe and the cancan for Paris, and for New York, a street-fight. Fortunately, London did not feature.

10 *Black Humour: The Threepenny Opera*

L
ondon, Soho, 1899. Con man, Mr J.J. Peachum, runs an emporium, exclusively for the outfitting of beggars. He disciplines, clothes and programs them in street manners which enable them to obtain without the use of force maximum charity. To a freeloader who has just been brought into the fold after being chastised, he explains the five basic categories of misery and displays the clothing suited to each. In return for being initiated, dressed-up for the appropriate stratagem and allocated a territory, this new recruit need only hand-over one half of all his future takings to the entrepreneurial Peachum.

This is the first demoralising scene in *The Threepenny Opera*, an entertainment designed for the imagination of beggars, and of a cost and quality to match. An announcement to this effect has interrupted an orchestral prelude just as it is breaking into a fugue in the style of 18th century baroque, but slightly run-down, a poor man's Bach.

This cut-price opera is accompanied by no more than seven musicians, versatile enough on their instruments to resemble a jazz band, and sometimes sounding like one. A street singer will comment dead-pan on the deeds of gangster 'Captain' Macheath, known as Mac the Knife, starting with a little song[1] with barrel-organ accompaniment to which banjos soon add some pace. Macheath is to be the anti-hero and Peachum his prime antagonist, in a story of evil against evil.

Peachum delivers a sermon with harmonium accompaniment to his large assembly of beggars, in unctuous language to bring them further into line. Peace is disturbed when his wife arrives distraught, to announce that Macheath has run off with their daughter Polly. But why should her disappearance ruin Peachum financially? Did he intend to sell her once, or several times? Love cannot frustrate his plans in the long run and he takes consolation in verses which support his view. The romantic dream is expressed in the image of the Moon over Soho.

It will soon be apparent to what extent Macheath is seeking respectability, though for the wedding, a stable is a singular choice, and he is no Jesus. His mobsters have requisitioned furniture for the occasion, with such zeal that someone has been killed. Substituting for bridesmaids, the gang sing what sounds like a chorus of dead-beats. To a funeral dirge, the bridal pair speak touchingly of never being separated and sing a passionless duet in very slow waltz-time. Polly raises spirits with a lusty tale of a hotel menial who suffers daily humiliation from the rich citizens but who will take command when her pirate confederates seize the town, chopping off the heads of anyone who has offended her.

Mac's corrupt police confederate, 'Tiger' Brown, is the guest of honour pleased to attend the wedding and they sing the terse, energetic *Canon duet,* how they present their notions of army heroics, with impressions in the accompaniment of how two ignorant chauvinists might have perceived non-European civilisations. Brown then rushes off to attend his duties at the Royal event, from which Macheath is destined in mystical fashion to benefit gratuitously.

After the wedding night, Polly persuades him to go into hiding, and he makes her deputy leader of the gang. With his departure, she asserts her authority, cutting a recalcitrant underling down to size; there is steel within her, perhaps explaining in part why she has has undertaken this marriage.

Returned home, she makes clear to her parents the masochistic nature of her new passion, impersonating in song a certain Barbara, who rejected many presentable lovers in favour of a fascinatingly evil man. His special appeal was that he offered nothing.

Whenever it serves his material advantage Polly's father is strong on religious imagery, and she is due a lengthy dissertation on human frailty. Regardless of the environment, act one operatic finales should be up-beat, even if only to keep the show going, so the family join in, throwing off dejection. The music takes on a frantically cheerful aspect, increasing in pace with startling thematic changes, the scene ending abruptly to unresolved chords. The audience is left in suspense.

Polly has a presentiment of disaster; her moon has lost its fullness and its glow, she knows of Mac's crimes, but in her loneliness she will stand by him. Mrs Peachum had been deceived by Macheath's genteel pose, but is now bribing his previous *inamorata*, Jenny, to turn him in. They seal their compact by singing *The Ballad of Sexual Dependency*, to an insistent slow beat and a doleful saxophone, reflecting on the cause of Mac's imminent downfall. This precedes a scene in a brothel, which is Mac's favourite haunt for business and pleasure and where he meets Jenny who is intent on a final betrayal; in music which evokes a louche those-were-the-days world, they sing a cynical duet detailing how Macheath had lived off her immoral earnings. Then the Judas act and the kiss. She signals the police to close in.

The brothel scene has built up to a powerful climax, perfectly suited to bring the curtain down though it is situated formally in the middle of the second act. The Old Bailey prison scene which follows is fuelled by female rage; such a desirable man is certain to be fought over by women, but incompetent 'Tiger' Brown is ignorant of daughter Lucy's secret marriage to his friend Mac. The meeting of the two 'wives' at the prison releases music of vituperation in what the narrator in detached Brechtian terms calls a 'struggle for property'. With a strident aria of jealousy, Lucy plays the fine lady in declamation punctuated by Polly's street repartee, a comical operatic burlesque. When the girls pause for breath, they share a delicate interlude in close harmony, rapturous in their love of the same man.

Mac sings a euphoric ballad about the easy life – freedom is less important than comfort. He tries to evade the women's quarrel before making a tactical switch in Lucy's favour, Polly is dragged off by her mother, and the pregnant Lucy considers all the melodramatic means of achieving an escape. Having thoughtfully stuffed a pillow under her dress, she can effect this by pretending to be in labour, so distracting the jailer.

A splendidly theatrical opportunity is at hand, a coronation. Sadly, this is no *Boris Godunov* and *The Threepenny Opera* has neither the wish nor the space to celebrate such flummery. It is casually used only as a mechanism in the plot, and by Peachum.

Being aware of 'Tiger' Brown's disposition, Peachum reminds him of the torture inflicted on the police chief who failed to prevent a mob disrupting Queen Semiramis' cortège. If Brown does not seize Macheath, the multitude of London's beggars will be set loose on the royal occasion. This is Peachum's *coup*; in agonies of conscience, 'Tiger' is obliged to act.

This has been a most hectic second act, so its finale may be more reflective, a cheerless parable, in frozen time; under a spot-light, Mac and Jenny think on the desperation of people striving to remain alive, even casting aside their humanity; anguished harmonies to a funeral march.

Act III begins with agreeably light-hearted music reflecting on human inadequacy. These must be the final moments of frivolity before the solemn proceedings commence which should lead to retribution. Lucy celebrates her role in Mac's betrayal with her *Solomon song*. This is a heavy barrel-organ dirge, recalling famed characters of antiquity who have fallen from grace – even wise Solomon, with 300 wives, must have had a problem. Cleopatra, Caesar, and now Macheath are listed among those brought low by sensual delights.

Under constraint, Mac's personality is transformed as he sees himself as some kind of holy man, speaking from a symbolic grave, then in a monotone epitaph on the way to the gallows has the arrogance to offer forgiveness and salvation to the whole of society except the police.

Opera is an artificial entity, so the audience should not become too involved. Alienation will enable them to accept an alternative ending, a more entertaining one?

Mac is no fall guy. He has been laying plans to graduate to a more profitable form of crime – banking!! Now privilege will be seen to triumph over justice, and Her Majesty is merciful to the favoured. *Deus ex machina.* To mark the Coronation, her messenger arrives to a galloping rhythm, 'Tiger' Brown on a pantomime horse, with a joyful announcement; Mac will be rewarded for his enterprise and, in the noble spirit of the past, join the nobility, be given a fine residence and an annuity sufficient to make him feel comfortable among the ruling classes.

The beggars are permitted to join in a Lutheran chorale which rises climactically; then the street-singer repeats his theme-song, accepting with equanimity the accepted moral climate . . . . . . some live in the light and some in the dark.

Pirate Jenny is often performed out of context, a fine dramatic monologue original in style. The anxious first theme of the *Barbara song* pointedly distorts a popular melody, *I'm only a wandering vagabond*, composed in the 1920s for an escapist Berlin operetta[2].

The *Barbara song's* second theme seems to be taken straight from the best-known of Russian melodies, *Otchi Chornia* (Black Eyes), which has appeared in many appealing guises for over a century. Here it is passionate and immensely nostalgic, acting as a recurring love theme; it is quoted again at the end of the brothel scene, just as a policeman puts a hand on Mac's shoulder, a neat allusion to love betrayed.

The basic story and the main characters of *The Threepenny Opera* were extracted by Bertolt Brecht from the *Beggars' Opera*. This was a musical whose first text, by John Gay for a London production in 1728, satirised contemporaneous life and politicians. By using popular melodies of the time, it presented a burlesque on the obscurities and artificialities of opera written to Italian texts. This was so effective that George Handel's stage works lost their vogue, his business suffered badly and he was obliged to start composing no less successful operas in English.

Brecht's satire has far different purposes. It is more generalised and, in the revisions he subsequently made, increasingly directed at the nature of capitalistic societies. Many people found the text offensive, some thought it blasphemous and one lead actress refused to sing *The Ballad of Sexual Dependency*.

For composer Weill, this was an experimental work, the major aim being to write a 'serious' musical which moved as far as possible away from traditional opera, especially of the grander variety. He called it 'the most consistent reaction to Wagner ... the complete destruction of the concept of music drama.' Nostalgia replaces passion, and the music expresses no concern for the tragedy being enacted, a significant parallel to Brecht's alienation effect in the drama. Similarly, the music negates the euphony and optimism of 20th century romantic musicals.

Formally, operatic style and conventions are ignored, and the original players were selected as actors who could sing just a little, in popular or folk style, the music scored to meet their limitations. Far more than in modern operas, action remains suspended during the songs which often have sharply ironic effect, such as negating the language of the love songs. In style, they resemble traditional ballads, cabaret songs or dance numbers, but eccentric in their use of fragmented melodies, banal rhythms and disorienting harmonies. The pervading irony of music often out of spirit with its lyrics is thrown into relief by listening to the spirited orchestral suite later made from the music.

The Threepenny Opera appealed to different kinds of audience simultaneously, which helps to explain its extraordinary success in the four years before the Nazis had the power to ban it. To them, it was an example of 'decadent art', and its pessimistic view of human nature displeased the German Communist party, though the work was to become admired from the USSR to the USA. It was not performed in Britain for many years, perhaps out of the stage world's loyalty to *The Beggars' Opera.*

The Theater am Schiffbauerdamm, Berlin, where *The Threepenny Opera* was first performed, became after the war home of the famous Berliner Ensemble, subsidised by the East German state. Brecht was in charge there until his death in 1956, but his policies were continued and it remained a centre for social challenge.

The anarchic spirit of *The Threepenny Opera*[3] now makes it appear a characteristic expression of 1920s' dissidence in Germany, and that aspect was promptly applauded by several leading critics. Herbert Jhering commented in 1928 that it was:

'... the break-through of a type of theatre that is not oriented towards chic society ... the tone neither opposes nor negates morality, it does not attack norms but transcends them ... it proclaims a different world in which the barriers between tragedy and humour have been erased.'

11   *Rossini and Opera Buffa*

Italy had the best known tradition of stage humour in Europe, back to the Renaissance, especially the *commedia dell'arte*, based upon well-loved stereotyped characters. These became part of a popular culture, enlivened by the constant improvisations of the actors. Early plots often involved a young man, played by a soubrette (light soprano), and a gullible old woman, a comic (*buffo*) role for male voice. More elaborate forms evolved; the more familiar comic trio might include the skittish Harlequin, charming Colombine and elderly Pantaloon. These three would fit respectively into a musical pattern of tenor, prima *buffa* (soprano) and primo *buffo* (deep-voiced and the object of ridicule, hence the English term buffoon). What we still call the Clown was a later addition.

Opera *seria* often had comic interludes, involving some of the characters, or the servants of the protagonists. The interludes became enlarged and detached, so opera *buffa* came into its own, normally with three or four entertainers, and was well established by the 18th century. It was greatly enhanced in certain works by Mozart, *The Marriage of Figaro* and *Cosi fan tutte* calling for six principal singers, and the genre gradually became more popular than Italian opera *seria* which was declining in quality. Rossini breathed some fresh life into opera *seria*, but that was almost the end. The new fashion which was taking Italian and other opera houses by storm from the 1820s was romantic opera, most of which were tragic and broke the earlier tradition of the 'happy ending'; yet they could also be in the spirit of opera *buffa*, such as Donizetti's *Don Pasquale* (based on a story with a 'Pantaloon' in a comic trio) and *The Daughter of the Regiment*, and Verdi's *Falstaff*.

Rossini was one of very few great composers who could write intrinsically funny music; that and his sense of drama go far to explain the continued success of his *buffo* operas, of which at least three are often in British repertoires.

Of these, *The Barber of Seville* and *The Italian Girl in Algiers* have plots where resourceful heroines comfortably outwit presumptuous males in the course of comical music confrontations.

Marilyn Horne, one of the greatest singers of the century of recorded music, with immense power in the lower range and encompassing at least two and one half octaves, has recorded humorous songs, from Handel to fellow American, Aaron Copland. As a Rossini specialist, she has a particular interest in *L'Italiana in Algeri*, (The Italian Girl), written in 1813 by the 21 year-old Rossini.

The plot centres on the heroine Isabella seeking to rescue her lover, Lindoro, who is held incognito as servant to Mustafa, Bey of Algiers. Shrugging off the attentions of a travelling admirer, she commands him for added protection to pose as her 'uncle', a comic figure, later trading insults with her whenever jealousy overcomes him.

Next to be put down is Mustafa, said to be 'the scourge of women' in a jaunty chorus with eunuchs anticipating an easy triumph for their master. To Isabella, he is just another ineffectual male, and even if she finds him the handsomest on stage, his huge moustache and fancy headwear reduce him to a figure of ridicule. They instantly exchange highly personal comments, she often repeating *Che muzo* (What a mug), whilst he gloats *Che pezzo da sultano* (Just ripe for a sultan).

Tension increases when Lindoro arrives, more astonished than overjoyed by his lover's presence. With Isabella completely self-possessed, the two suitors and four courtiers are transfixed, then to exaggerated gestures, join an ensemble of confusion. This has a complexity and rhythic intensity never previously achieved in *buffo* style, and one in which Marilyn Horne has often performed and considers the funniest of its kind in all opera.

Because Mustafa is attempting to marry his unwanted wife off to Lindoro, Isabella incites rebellion in the harem, a comic notion previously given an outing in Mozart's *Seraglio* *(1782)*.

Italian sailors at the port are irresolute, so Isabella takes over, steeling them to prepare for an escape; if Mustafa can be lured into one of their boats, they can set sail, letting him jump off or swim for it. The familiar entrapment device is to work on the victim's self-esteem, offering him initiation into a prestigious secret society, in this case the non-existent Italian *Pappatacci*. To a mock ceremony and on-stage band, the ensuing *buffo* trio is a show-stopper.

Miss Horne relishes the chance to embellish freely on the melodic repeats, her deep-ranging voice even adding a top C; in Rossini's time, but not much later, singers might have their own phrases from which to select. There was even more scope for improvisation in the dialogues, especially in a work like this which is a variant of *commedia dell'arte* set to music.

■ ■ ■

The Journey to Rheims goes nowhere, but does so in style, an operatic show-piece which is not an opera. It had been commissioned by King Charles X of France on accession, to celebrate his coronation at the traditional location, Rheims Cathedral, in 1825. For this, Rossini composed what he called a scenic cantata, his last stage work in the Italian language, prepared for Paris' Théâtre-Italien, to be performed by the finest soloists available.

He took a rare opportunity to compose operatic melodies and ensembles unrestricted by dramatic needs, bel canto for its own sake, drawing on his mastery of both opera *buffa* and *seria*. It was a virtuoso work, but adding musical comments on contemporaneous styles.

Rossini at that time was widely celebrated as the greatest living composer, certainly of opera, but was particularly conscious of a new movement in the arts, Romanticism. He was worried that it might rapidly displace him, and though he treated it humorously in *The Journey to Rheims*, it became a major factor in his decision to retire from composing operas four years later. What emerged was a work for connoisseurs, a burlesque enjoying symbolism and sophisticated allusions, but too subtle for a bored King.

The excessive demands it would make on any commercial theatre company were prohibitive; 15 principal singers were too costly without royal patronage. King Charles did not survive the 1830 revolution, and Rossini permitted the cannibalising of the original score for the nuptials of the Austrian Emperor in 1855.

It is only very recently that *The Journey to Rheims* has been with much research reassembled, gaining in critical esteem and earning a commercial recording award. Of its set-piece arias, some have an element of self-parody, others progressing towards more adventurous styles of expression; in part a period piece with what now sounds like a quaint view of national attitudes to life and music.

Some features of an operatic performance are unnecessary, such as the distinct acts originally specified. The stage can be arranged functionally and without scenes to be changed, with brief interludes after virtuoso arias and other highlights sufficing.

The scenario is a cosmopolitan gathering of cultured persons, on their way to Rheims, which they will not reach. The Overture merges, *buffo* style, into a bantering exchange between housekeeper and the hotel staff, on edge at the impending arrival of distinguished guests. She spells out the technique of flattery:

> 'The Contessa is to be humoured; she is always impatient for action. Talk to the Chevalier about beautiful women: to the Muscovite about the vast Empire: to the Roman about the Capitol: to the German about counterpoint. With art, ingenuity and our native talents, like a flooding torrent, the noble fame of the Inn of the Golden Lily will spread to every shore.'

The announcement that the carriage which is to take the party to Rheims has collapsed sets-up a diverting chain reaction. This fashion-conscious French Contessa, her new clothes damaged in the accident, walks on dressed in nothing but the French tricolour, and appears to die in operatic manner. The doctor diagnoses syncope, which sounds more more impressive than a fainting fit, and the German Baron misreads this as 'syncopation'. The orchestra obliges him by demonstraing with excerpts from Bach, Mozart, Haydn and Beethoven.[1]

That revives the Contessa who sings coloratura of a severe moral dilemma facing her, one too appalling to be articulated and which 'only the ladies would understand'. It concerns an impediment to her attending the coronation, and she invokes God's aid. When a bonnet in the latest Paris fashion flies through the auditorium and comes to hand, it solves her problem, a sign not just from God but several of them addressed in an exultant cabaletta.

The Baron is citing her as an example of the irrational human condition when a Polish Marchesa, commanding in contralto voice which might restrain the ardour of men, arrives on the arm of Don Alvaro and pursued by a jealous Russian Count. Frenchmen would have seen a political parable here, the Russians continuing to covet and occupy Poland after the departure of its protector, Napoleon. A large, heavily cloaked bass-baritone resembles the Imperial Russian bear, but the Polish lady, with French sentiment on her side, resists.

The Russian challenges his rival to a duel, but by-standers intervene and a noble sextet develops with superbly measured pace. This is interrupted by a soothing off-stage harp and the 'improvisation' of the poetess Corinna, who looks down, a muse of harmony. Becalmed by her benediction, they form a tableau of unity, national colours prominent, and sing in human fellowship.

Pure love is represented by a youthful English Lord, overwhelmed by the remote Corinna. He is introduced by a virtuoso flute solo, suited once to accompany all manner of distress, but rather long and florid for our times. This lyric tenor, too shy to confess his love for Corinna, hides his feelings behind the artificiality of opera *seria* whilst a chorus of flower-maidens encourage him to make offering to the exalted poetess.

Having descended to the world of mortals, she has to struggle for her honour, threatened by a French Chevalier. He believes that women's resistance is a matter of form: today no, tomorrow yes! Operatic heroines should not be involved in scuffles and she takes refuge with her harp. The beauty of her song briefly enters into close harmony with his, so the signs are once more misread: just another operatic tenor trying it on.

Don Procopio has a passion for the past, which goes well with voguish Romanticism and is fascinated by the culture of the British Isles which was making an immense impact on literary Europe. He asks where he may find relics of Ossian and King Arthur, but the Lord is a Philistine, brusquely suggesting a museum.

Corinna is gently ridiculed throughout: she is a lady who 'wants to be alone', standing on a pedestal for most of the time, but she is also a literary conceit, an example of the 'new woman'. The 1820s were a period when assertions of female rights were thought outrageous.

Corinna also represents the new literary Romanticism, whereas Rossini's musical style was of the immediate past, late classical; though in his final opera, *William Tell*, he moved expressively in the new direction.

His characteristic patter songs are for a deep male voice and often go well with secretive business. Don Procopio peeps into the trunks of the travellers who are prepared to depart and finds what he expected: the Spaniard carries details of family trees and valued mementos of the Americans: the Pole literary classics and artefacts: the French lady, jewellery and the appurtenances of love: the German, musical treatises and strange-sounding brass instruments: the Englishman nautical documents, China tea, opium, air-guns and IOUs: the Frenchman lithographs, painted shells and billets doux: the Russian precious sables and maps to explore Siberia or conquer Turkey.

The Don is being questioned by the volatile Contessa about the Chevalier's philanderings when news arrives: no alternative transport to Rheims is available, so the coronation will be missed.

This causes general distress, starting with a heart-rending *a capella* passage, the singers without orchestral accompaniment reaching out to the audience in more intimate manner[2] until the orchestra enters with a relaxed, swaying melody in 3–4 time.

A letter received from the capital announces that festivities will continue there for several days after the coronation, so the Contessa invites them all to stay at her Paris home. These decisions occur within a powerful ensemble to form a *scena* in three parts. This is a tour de force for 14 soloists, a 'grand concertante piece', and of proportions never previously attempted with success by any composer. The celebration reaches a climax in the 'let's go' section, to an exceptionally vigorous tempo, balancing two jubilant melodies.

The remaining *contretemps* has to be resolved. The Russian's words of love are too effusive, the heroic language of grand opera; he cannot adjust to the Marchesa's teasing, but she brings his suffering to an end in a love duet romantically 'overheated'. It looks to the future when a young Verdi would compose music more fiery and decreasingly ornamental.

A staged divertissement will complete the final evening at the Inn, starting with a troupe of dancing marionettes. Their jerky movements mock the latest trends in ballet, though the music is charmingly light and with compulsive rhythms. This is how Rossini would compose for *soirées musicales* among friends during some 40 years of retirement, his self-styled 'sins of old age'.

Each guest is to propose a song to represent his country. The choice sounds trite to modern ears and over-dignified with a large chorus. In the 1820s, knowledge in refined musical circles of national styles was minimal, a matter of little interest and no commercial value. This naïve theatrical display purports to serve the cause of international brotherhood.

There are two national anthems, the British chosen by the Lord whilst the German selects Haydn's *Emperor* melody, then linked with the Austrian monarchy. Castanets and a melody which prefers to stay with one note suggest Spain and the Russian contribution, said to be a hymn, sounds Italianate[3] Most easily identified would have been the polonaise, the Marchesa lunging with a sword, a head-long rhythmic effect which was assumed to typify Polish dancing; whilst the tiresome Chevalier is reconciled with the Contessa as they represent their country in a sentimental old romance, *Charmante Gabrielle*.

The hostess is to wind-up the entertainment. This she does in company with Don Profondo, setting up a powerful beat to keep the chorus in line, combining commerce with politics, praising the Golden Lily and France's destiny. As the *fleur de lis* was the emblem of King Charles' dynasty, this is flattery suitable for the opera's patron.

There is to be a draw for which one of France's historical figures is to be celebrated; Joan of Arc, St Louis and several other names are entered, but the ballot box is transparent and King Charles' name is selected. Corinna is asked to lead the chorus of praise, which she does in fine bel canto style, giving a show of false modesty when she utters that cliché of Italian opera: *Io tremo* (I tremble with fear).

A pantomime King Charles is admitted to the auditorium,

standing on a plinth for the grand finale, based upon a popular song in praise of his ancestor, Henri IV.

The composer was always economical with his material, and much of this was used again, three years later in *Count Ory*, though sadly not the sextet ... Like so many operas developed from a text by Eugene Scribe, it combines comedy and romance.

■ ■ ■

Count Ory is a tale of the era when the pillaging of the crusaders was matched by the lechery of the men who stayed at home. As chastity belts never existed, noble ladies used to seek collective security within castles which, with their retinues, they were entrusted to maintain. It tells how one young lady, Adèle , who is left in charge by her brother, resists the outlandish attempts of the wandering Count Ory to seduce her.

He and his followers are so disreputable that his father has despatched a force to seize him, which is why he travels incognito. He appears spying out Adèle 's territory in the guise of a saintly hermit, wearing a halo and mouthing comforting platitudes as if he were an astrologer. This charms the local maidens so much that, to music which barely suppresses sexual ardour, they sublimate feelings by idolising him.

Adèle is keen to seek his spiritual guidance because she is suffering from nervous depression, and even suspects that this is a consequence of a vow of virginal chastity. She is experiencing the first pangs of sexual frustration, so to everyone's pleasure, in the name of Heaven the 'holy' man releases her from the vow.

The immediate beneficiary appears to be her cousin, Isolier, who is more honourable in his desire for her, and Ory's misery is complete when his father's men find and denounce him outside the castle. In a septet taken from the biggest ensemble of *The Journey to Rheims*, a powerful conflict of emotions concludes the first act as Isolier is welcomed into the castle.

The second act unfurls to a wonderfully relaxed motif for the only scene free from male scheming. This occurs as the women take baths in seclusion, an extended choral *scena* of the kind which would find great favour in romantic opera. It is followed by a typical Rossini orchestral storm, heightening tension before the extended dénouement.

With barely two days before the crusaders and Adèle's fearsome brother are to arrive, Ory and his men have one final ploy. Dressed as nuns, they claim sanctuary in the castle from Ory's gang of rapists. Their prayer session lacks conviction and the game could be up with their frolics after drinking all the wine in the cellars. By the time Ory enters the lady's chamber, Isolier is cosily in bed with her. Because of the darkness, the villain's attempts at fondling are misdirected, but nothing can deny the magnificence of their trio, which Berlioz and others considered to be the greatest music Rossini ever wrote. The crusaders enter on pantomime horses to a brisk march, but are too exhausted to stop the intruders taking their time over a choral farewell.

Ory's role is scored for an unusually high tenor voice, just one of many comic devices with which the work is loaded – exaggerated gestures, absurd disguises, asides, voices in the falsetto range, swooning maidens, prancing nuns; the Adèle -Ory-Isolier plot is structured like a harlequinade. Yet Adèle's music reveals a passionate nature, whilst the two men feel intensely behind the buffoonery. Between opera and farce, *Count Ory* is a comic masterpiece, and Rossini's farewell to opera *buffa*.

12 *An Italian Falstaff*

In *Falstaff,* Verdi finally put aside themes of war, political ambition, rebellion, heroism and passion, in favour of action at the domestic level: a conflict between men and women of property and those intending to deprive them of it; the diplomacy of the boudoire, the urge for revenge, the assumed lechery of older men and the romantic idealism of youth.

In masterly characterisation, Verdi sketches a favourite Shakespeare character, Sir John Falstaff, once debonaire but reduced as time passes by his need for money, self-esteem, and the regard of women. In the two plays which comprised *Henry IV,* Falstaff, drinking companion of the Crown Prince, employs dishonest means to support his debauched habits, but in *The Merry Wives of Windsor,* the humour is turned against him in counter-actions which succeed in teaching him an overdue lesson.

This play would appear to be unpromising operatic material: a sprawling plot with a confusion of characters, the appeal lying not in any literary excellence but in a sequence of comic incidents, jokes and bawdy phrases. This unsubtle work was commissioned by Queen Elizabeth because of her delight in the character of Falstaff, but was certain to pull large audiences.

Yet Shakespeare presents his popular comic hero unfavourably, perhaps a protest at being obliged to write the play. It might have been suitably trimmed, to make an operetta plot, and its most successful adaptation before Verdi is still widely performed in Germany: Otto Nicolai's *Merry Wives of Windsor (1849).* This version eliminates Falstaff's disreputable drinking companions, Pistol, Nym and Bardolph. It is presented as a foolishly amorous tale, the opening scene centred on two married women who have received love letters from Falstaff simultaneously. The complex motivation leading up to this is unimportant against the action which follows.

Verdi would not have been influenced by the Nicolai,

excellent though it is. In contrast, Verdi gave it an entirely operatic treatment, action often concurrent with arias, and he was perfectly served by his librettist, Arrigo Boito, who had once left off composing operas to prepare an inspired text for their previous collaboration, *Otello.*

Boito, with a deep understanding of Shakespeare, reduced the original play to desirable operatic proportions, and included lyrics drawn from Italian literature. There is no necessity to locate the play in time and place; this is a timeless music drama.

A complex story is covered at very rapid pace, six scenes of some twenty minutes each. The townsfolk with complaints against Falstaff and the rich suitors for young Nanetta are combined in one person, the elderly Doctor Caius, most unlike Shakespeare's fiery character. Nanetta Ford's true lover remains Fenton, a light romantic tenor role, with glowing lyrical moments for the two young persons.

Verdi's expressive powers worked to their most concentrated effect, the musical themes very fertile but used sparingly, aria and recitative integrated. Unlike traditional Italian opera, there is a minimum of melodic repetition.

A striking example of the economy of Verdi's late musical style is given by Charles Osborne, an authority on the composer. In *Henry IV*, Falstaff pays eloquent tribute to the red nose of his companion, Bardolph, with a comparison to Hellfire. Osborne admires the tuneful phrase which Verdi gives Falstaff (*tuo naso ardentissimo*) which is not heard again. He suggests it would have been good enough to last Puccini for a whole aria, and perhaps did.[1]

In this final work for the stage, 1893, Verdi reflects on the style and idiosyncrasies of Italian opera over the full half century he had worked within it, and enjoys making musical comments. With its moments also of self-parody and in-jokes, this is one of the wittiest of all comedy operas.

Without a prelude, the scene becomes increasingly turbulent in response to complaints that Falstaff's confederates, Pistol and Bardolph, have once more been 'coney-catching', winning the confidence of acquaintants or getting them drunk before robbing them. The victim, Doctor Caius, gets no redress from Falstaff who shields the two scoundrels. They reward this gesture by refusing to deliver two letters, no doubt because they are to receive no money up front, though they pretend to have moral objections. Provoked, Falstaff gives them an amoral sermon on the worthlessness of honour:[2]

'Ignominious cesspools, you stand upon your honour ... when even I am obliged to disregard my fear of God, and of necessity put honour aside in favour of deceit ... Can honour fill the stomach or mend a broken shoe, a foot, a limb? Honour is not a surgeon, so, what is it? A word. What's in this word? A puff of air. Can a dead man feel honour? Does it live only with the living? Flattery inflates it, pride corrupts it and calumny poisons it. I want none of it.'

This is delivered in semi-recitative with fulsome gestures, the rich imagery enhanced by the instruments. Previously, the praise he had laid on the two Windsor housewives was exposed as hypocrisy by Bardolph and Pistol, who are sharp enough to turn irony against him in an *Amen* chorus. Falstaff is exposed as planning to live off their rich husbands, so he justifies himself in fulsome rhetoric. The scene ends in musical rage as the two men find themselves at the rough, physical end and are driven out of the tavern. Their subsequent betrayal will contribute to his suffering two spectacular humiliations in succession, three in the Shakespeare play, though one of them would be superfluous for an opera.

The wives, Mistresses Ford and Page, cannot treat his letters as more than a joke and may doubt his sexual adequacy, believing that he may try to prove it. They never become aware of his real motivation, and he seems to be comparably deluded about the attractions of his person or knightly status.

The following scene catches the hilarity of the women's reactions on receiving the letters, saucy propositions rather than proposals and puffed out with poetic clichés. The contents are being discussed in detail, to the intense amusement of Nanetta Ford (Ann Page in Shakespeare), and the town gossip, Mistress Quickly. Alice Ford does not lack feminine guile, and is protected by a sense of fun which alone would ruin such a man's chances. She recites the letter written to her friend, Meg Page, with a mocking musical accompaniment which changes to gloriously romantic phrasing on the words:

Let's mate in blissful love, the beautiful lady and the man of distinction.

The ideal encounters the grotesque in this exquisite moment, and the women agree a spiky declaration of revengeful intent. That and the remainder of the scene are played out at a sparkling pace as Bardolph and Pistol, in hopes of speedy remuneration, join forces with Ford and Caius, all oblivious of the women's proximity; Falstaff's manoeuvres are betrayed.

What follows reduces the spectacular choruses of grand opera to an absurd contest between two vocal quartets thrown into startling rhythmic contrast, the mocking, measured tread of the women and the accelerating fury of the men. Nanetta finds time to flirt sweetly with her prospective lover in a Boccaccio quote which fits an idyllic duet of calf-love;

A mouth that is kissed is never unlucky. It renews itself like the moon.

The women crudely impersonate Falstaff in his fatness, then with dramatic change of tempo, Alice holds centre stage with a repetition of the rapturous *Let's mate in blissful love,* the scene rounded-off with a delicious burst of musical laughter.

What should be a cursory meeting follows, but blown up into an eccentric ritual, a piquant cameo referred to by its Italian key-word, *Reverenza,* a most respectful term of address. Mistress Quickly arrives at Falstaff's haunt to find him drinking, then delivers – but in a prolonged sequence of curtseys – an assignation from Mistress Ford, that he should call between two and three when her husband is at work. Falstaff responds gallantly to her bowing, exchanging courtesies matched by music of the richest insincerity. The phrase, *from two till three*, becomes a musical motif colouring the remainder of the scene.

Quickly is now so well tuned-in that she can with ease discharge a second message, that Meg Page is equally flattered but – *povera donna* (wretched lady) – she is less able to escape her husband's attentions. The phrase *povera donna* might be recognised as relating to the heroine of Verdi's *Traviata*, and is played by Quickly for all its comic theatricality. Falstaff accepts the bait, that women always enjoy such duplicity. Alone, he laughs at himself in song, *Get on, old John*, a very short-winded march for him to plod once more into some kind of battle.

Before he can think about the improbabilities, Ford is announced, posing as Signor Fontane, a man who desires Alice Ford but who has often been discouraged by her coldness. Would Falstaff, in return for instant delivery of champagne and a promised sum of money, warm her up, act the Pandar, so open a path for him?

Ford adopts several postures; flattery, male banter, a burlesque of a madrigal, but in asides shows the intense feeling which any reference to his wife provokes. Led on by bribes, Falstaff boasts that he is within 30 minutes of the ultimate success with Alice, and that the husband will soon be in Hell with his 'ancestor', Menelaus.

As Falstaff goes off to dress for action, this reference and the taunts about wearing horns have the effect that Ford can no longer disguise; his enraged soliloquy contains music which would not be misplaced in Verdi's *Otello (1882)*, and has a phrase which recalls one from *Don Carlos (1867)* in the scene where the King bitterly contemplates his loveless marriage.

The fury of Ford's sung monologue is the emotional peak of the whole work, with a superbly ironic contrast at the climax which releases a noble theme representing his self-image, idealistic and honourable. Yet there's no question of Ford being seen in heroic colours; the anguished music never escapes from its ironic context. It is interrupted by a flippant accompaniment to Falstaff's strutting return in all his preposterous finery. The two men walk off in feigned *bonhomie*.

At Alice's home, Nanetta throws a tantrum at being ordered by her father to marry 'grandfather Caius', but once her mother reassures her, the women break into a joyous ensemble. They are preparing to administer a searing indignity: Falstaff is to be ejected by laundry basket into the River Thames. Mistress Quickly causes great amusement in acting out the *Reverenza* scene.

Falstaff's arrival finds Alice mistress of the situation and able gently to counter his familiarities. He attempts a serenade, not enhanced by voice, age or girth, but confidently promises jewels, a coat of arms, and the title of Lady through marriage when, as he hopes, Ford dies. He recalls life at court as a once-slender page, nimble-footed, then attempts to show off in an aria of special delicacy, perhaps the briefest in all romantic opera.

This quaint flirtation is ended by a warning that Ford is approaching with several men in support. By the time they are searching the house, the victim is squeezed into the basket, sat upon and despatched through the window into the water below. The scene dissolves in comic polyphony, the women in skittish mood, the males in vexed confusion, and the two lovers occasionally floating their voices above the mêlée.

In the original play, Falstaff confides this episode to the still unrecognised Ford, but a second meeting would have been operatically ineffectual, especially after Ford's incomparable monologue. Instead, at the start of the following scene, Falstaff is sitting alone, filled with water and self-pity. A rumbling scherzo-like theme which was heard during the warning about Ford's arrival dominates a brief prelude. It also reflects Falstaff's confusions as he rationalises the situation: a fundamentally good man surrounded by *uno mondo ladro,* a world of thieves.

Orchestral trills describe the effects of wine passing through the veins and reviving his spirits. He has learned nothing from this venture, but another lesson will be similarly contrived, this time by the women with help from the town-folk.

Whilst still drenched from the ducking, Sir John receives the most unlikely visitor, Mistress Quickly. She even attempts to resume the *Reverenza* sequence but Falstaff has had his fill of her games.

Wounded pride induces him to swallow the fresh bait, that Alice really desires him. If he is prepared to revive an ancient ritual by appearing disguised as the deceased Black Hunter, at a lonely spot during festivities in Windsor Forest, she will find a pretext to bring them together in seclusion.

This time, the women are close at hand to enjoy the exchanges. They compile a mock requiem to the deceased hunter, then Alice conjures up an atmosphere of terror, indulging the women's ghostly fantasies. The music here recalls scenes from Verdi's *Ballo in Maschera*: the witch's fatal prediction, and the bantering dialogue between the King and Oskar.

At the designated time, Falstaff appears, dressed precisely as instructed and weighed down by two enormous antlers. His superstitions will make him look even more ridiculous because he believes that fairies arrive at midnight and should not be looked upon by humans. Countless revellers will be lurking in fancy dress; the chimes suggest impending doom, and Falstaff looks like a sacrificial victim.

He is allowed no more than a teasing moment with Alice then Nanetta with an escort of children performs enchantingly as Queen of the Fairies, graced by the delicacy and impishness of the music. Falstaff is protecting himself from magic spells by burying his head in the ground, but is discovered and terrified by creatures of the forest, all in masks, before having sense kicked into him by his male acquaintants.

He recovers just in time to put a good face on his ordeal. Conflict must be laid to rest, and a fresh perspective, social and optimistic, is to prevail, recalling a comparable reconciliation scene in *The Marriage of Figaro*. The finale ends in the most unexpected form, a choral fugue which would be Verdi's chosen farewell to opera.

Alice fulfils a promise, approving Fenton's betrothal to Nanetta, with Caius acknowledging his own inadequacy as a suitor. The merry but virtuous wives have won the day, but Falstaff quickly adjusts his vision; it has all been an entertainment with himself as the catalyst, the fountain of wit and humour. He concludes with a notion familiar elsewhere in Shakespeare: all the world is a stage, in fact, a joke.

13 *An English Falstaff*

Sir Edward Elgar was often interested in humorous subjects for composition, but recognised his own limitations[1], where he had a special regard for Ralph Vaughan Williams' apparently natural abilities in that direction. This was how he came to suggest that his younger colleague should set to music the racy, scurrilous verses of poet, John Skelton. The idea was taken up, resulting in the masterly *Five Tudor Portraits* which ranged from a description of a boozy, blowsy woman presiding over disorderly village goings-on to a mocking obituary for an unpopular local official. Vaughan Williams employed a forthright, modern symphonic style spiced with harmonic and rhythmic features from 15th century music.

Both men decided to present episodes in the life of Sir John Falstaff, Elgar's symphonic study creating a nobler character in an idealised Elizabeth England. Vaughan Williams reflected on several fine versions in music, including Verdi's which he considered incomparable, whilst Otto Nicolai's operetta-like *Merry Wives of Windsor* was a favourite with him. This is to a text which treats more lightly the relations between Falstaff and the stranger who wants to possess Alice Ford, with their comic duet which is still popular in Germany.

Unlike Nicolai and Verdi, Vaughan Williams retained Shakespeare's sub-plots in detail, stating that he wanted 'the whole crazy gang' to be included, a total of no fewer than 20 soloists. This meant presenting Falstaff with his warts, where Verdi's portrait was of a relatively vigorous and genial man.

Such a large-scale work went against the trend of the more flippant 1920s when there was also a broad reaction against the use of vast stage and musical resources which had been the norm in pre-war Europe. His stage play was to include lyrics to be selected from distinguished writers mainly of the 17th century. Performances of English operas were rare in the early 20th century, when critics raised eyebrows at any attempt to adapt folk music. Of this he used beautiful examples, but sparingly so that despite the period atmosphere created, the melodies are mainly his own, and excellent parodies. The dancing was to be in down-to-earth country-style, far from ballet.

Vaughan Williams could not be anything but an original, modestly setting, not following fashions. He was reacting against the spirit of Wagner which had been such an influence in opera for nearly a century. Yet this work has a powerful symphonic score, developing motifs, such as those relating to Falstaff's intended seductions and the four-note phrase for his love letters.

The selected title, *Sir John in Love*, has a touch of irony, as Queen Elizabeth I had wanted to see a play in which he was genuinely infatuated, but was denied the pleasure. By making play simultaneously for two women friends, Falstaff is a buffoon rather than lover or lecher. In his own image, he remains the male hunter.

He appears first in flippant mood, a suitable guise considering he is about to be implicated by a justice of the peace for criminal acts, then sweeps aside complaints against his associates and quickly leaves the scene.

The first act, taking place in a Windsor street, presents most of the characters of the play in several short scenes. To strident polyphony and sharp rhythmic changes, a clamorous gallery of men is heard. There are three suitors for the hand of Ann Page (Verdi's Nanetta Ford), who appears to the accompaniment of the exquisite folksong, *A Sailor from the Sea*, then a rapturous duet is shared with her young lover, Fenton.

This will be heard again to choral accompaniment when the couple are betrothed at the end of the play. Anti-climax follows. Doctor Caius is a rival suitor, but as absurd as in Shakespeare. He has an atrocious command of English grammar, which is far less tolerable in a supposed academic than a foreign accent. 17th century audiences, unfamiliar with anyone from the other side of the English Channel, would know how to treat a stereotyped Frenchman, irascible and foolishly passionate about love. The Doctor struts and blusters, already jealous about Ann whom, with the help of bribery and her mother, he is rashly confident of winning. He threatens to cut up Parson Evans, who is no more than an intermediary for a rival suitor, the young Slender.

A recurring orchestral motif deprives Caius of all dignity which he cannot regain when pressing his suit for Ann Ford, when he attempts to sing in courtly fashion. This has gently sliding melodic intervals, and sounds 'effete' in contrast with the gusty leaps of the prevailing English folk style[2].

Vaughan Williams composed a lusty drinking song for Falstaff's three companions as they reappear with freshly acquired loot. They are told by Falstaff of his plan to 'make thrift', that is, to scrounge off the wives and their husbands; but they realise it is time to find new allies and are set on betraying him. Their warning Ford about the threat to his wife pushes him into a deceit which will expose and punish Falstaff.

Meg Page has a more important singing role compared with that in the Verdi work where she is a foil to Alice Ford. The two wives are first heard, off-stage, mocking the opposite sex in a cuckoo's song, but the words are specially discomforting to the jealous Ford who is just out of sight.

The opera's title is reflected in the prominent orchestral motif from the folk song, *John, come kiss me now*; the irony is apparent when these words are sung in banter by the other men.

Falstaff's are received with some indignation by the wives, but by the time Mistress Page is quoting from the text, they are all ridiculing the sender. *Thine own true knight* is an obvious phrase to be mocked, and it forms the rhythmic basis to the lengthy discussion which follows after the text has been read in canon. Mistress Quickly introduces herself with *Lovely Joan*[3], a traditional song whose tranquil beauty contrasts with the bawdiness of its later verses. In the concluding trio, the women strike out in solidarity:

> *Sigh no more, ladies,*
> *Men were deceivers ever.*

The posturings of the adults give way briefly to youth enjoying the spring festivities. Fenton's lyricism overcomes Ann's token resistance after she has voiced her disapproval of his past association with the riotous Prince Henry; but he has also to win over her parents, each of whom favours an affluent suitor. The father's choice is the pathetic Slender, shy when addressing Ann but hoping to impress her with the sonnets he has been writing in sight of all.

Like Quickly, the Host is venal, but not without sympathy for young love; he tries to reassure Ann with a song about a happy wedding feast. He then sings of men's attitude to marriage, and the others join in at a rampant pace:

When I was a bachelor I lived a merry life
Now I am a married man and burdened with a wife. . . .[4]

The gloomy Ford is irritated and mocked by this thumping rhythm; and to the chimes, for ten o'clock,[5] he responds in grim recitative, inviting his confederates to a meal at his home, either to find 'the monster' or to celebrate his wife's fidelity.

Falstaff is comprehensively gulled during interviews with Quickly and Ford. She revels in intrigue, so Falstaff is easily flattered into believing he is certain of success with Alice. Sweeping the messenger into an improvised galliard, he calls on his muse: *Go thy ways, old Jack, I'll make more of my body than I ever have*, then sets about composing a song which he can dedicate to each lady. Snatches of it are also heard by the next visitor, Ford whom he has never seen and who can pose as a 'Mr Brook', lusting after Alice and asking for Falstaff's help.

As a bribe is included, Falstaff boasts that he will give the husband a pair of horns. This almost pushes the husband, briefly left alone, over the edge, an unhappy, alienated figure in his obsession with the word 'cuckold' which he keeps repeating.

The act ends in full orchestral bombast as Falstaff re-emerges resplendently dressed for wooing. At the Ford household, the final preparations by the women for Sir John's entrapment are completed just as he arrives to hear a welcoming rendering of *Greensleeves*, In confident, relaxed mood, he takes up the tune for a delectable moment as, imagining Alice asleep, he attempts to steal a kiss. Meg arrives on cue, with just time to stall Falstaff by exposing his duplicity; but with the alarm sounding for Ford's arrival, Falstaff's humiliation is compounded as he is forced to hide, squeezed into a laundry basket. The *Bachelor's* song has become a battle cry for the search party, lined up as if Falstaff is to run the gauntlet. This leads to a storming finale joined by a chorus of women who have the more cause for jubilation.

In the face of his wife's proven innocence, Ford is apologetic and prepared to listen to Meg Page's strategy for ensuring that Falstaff gets his final come-uppance. She explains how an old superstition about the Black Hunter of Windsor Forest will be put to good use.

This is effected during the final scene in the Forest where to trumpet sounds and an ominous version of the letter motif, Falstaff arrives, having complied with the conditions he must follow for a fresh assignation with Mistress Ford. The charade involves his dressing-up as the dead hunter in order to make love to her during the noisy diversion of a festival. He is still dwelling on his ducking in the river, but he reflects, the path of seduction is hazardous, and as Jupiter often proved, nothing helps more than disguise.

The voice of the Forest gives way to fairy music, but when hooded characters arrive, the music becomes boisterous, Falstaff being seized, thumped and pinched. A further part of the plan has been to disabuse the two hopeful suitors simultaneously, so with this achieved, Ford and the women will make their peace. Their final gesture is to approve the betrothal of Ann and Fenton who arrive to an off-stage chorus of Ben Jonson's anthem, *See the chariot at hand*.

A chastened Falstaff takes the lead, this time as the wise man and upholder of social mores:

> *Stand not amazed, here is no remedy.*
> *In love the heavens themselves do guide the state,*
> *Money buys land, and wives are sold by fate.*

In the concluding act, one hears the diversity of styles which are found in Vaughan Williams' most loved works: the turbulent and dramatic, the jocular, the lyrical and pastoral, an anthem which raises the spirits high. The concluding jig played by a bag-piper, *Half Hannikin'*, is a gem of its folksy kind.

14   *Humour and Richard Strauss*

'When did you compose *The Blue Danube?*' a poorly briefed newshound asked Richard Strauss on his final visit to England in 1947. The answer was 1867, when he was three years old, a German not related to Austria's most famous family or the actual composer, Johann Strauss II. Though journalists should know better, this coincidence of family name has always caused much confusion in Britain and the States.

This was increased by a sequence of waltzes written for Richard Strauss' opera, *Der Rosenkavalier*, comparable with the best by Johann and inspired by the Viennese tradition.

People still living who report meeting the elderly Strauss may not all have observed a marked sense of humour, but his was very important for his work, and he needed it often in social life. His wife Pauline with whom he shared a marriage over 50 years was known to intimidate visitors, including Nazis. Her personality was so strong that it occupied the centre space in an opera, *Intermezzo*, dramatising a jealous quarrel which had really occurred between the couple. He included a musical description of himself playing Skat, the South German card game which occupied much time when he was not composing about human drama and passions.

His inventiveness and virtuosity in orchestration took him to the point of claiming with justice he could describe anything he wished in music, from sophisticated human behaviour to commonplace objects. An early orchestral triumph had been *Till Eulenspiegel (1895)*, with descriptions of a young tearaway creating havoc both in a law court and a market place during a life which could only lead to the gallows. His execution was given realistic instrumentation.

Perhaps the greatest master of programme music, where humour plays a major part, in diverse symphonic works, he sketched the critics snarling at his work, his infant son being bathed, a windmill and flock of sheep being assailed by Don Quixote. All this brought protests that he had gone beyond the bounds of refined musical expression. Yet among his admirers, Neville Cardus wrote of the Quixotic episodes:

> *... one of music's best jokes. As an expression of mutton-headed stupidity, with the right herded immobility and vacancy of eye, this passage is sublimely comic ... Strauss in Don Quixote empties the entire contents of his orchestral box of tricks for our delight; he whirls the windmill round and round while the knight attacks, with poor Sancho making the most agitated protests.*

Conversations between Quixote and Panza are represented in dialogues for solo cello and viola; no surprise that a few years later, Strauss determined to conquer the musical theatre with such virtuosity. The first of his operas to embrace lengthy scenes which moved beyond comedy into outright farce was his fifth, *Der Rosenkavalier*; yet the work stands as a classic expression of romantic love in various critical phases. Strauss would say that Mozart's operas above all others held the key to the human heart; but his own contribution was immense.

Der Rosenkavalier contains supreme examples of musical irony. It uniquely combines the attractions of music drama and of operetta and is based on a play by the distinguished Austrian poet, Hugo von Hofmannsthal. That was self-sufficient as a work of art, often performed without music, and as a silent film.

Strauss was specially pleased because he had asked for a 'Mozartian' libretto, and this had in plot and mood some affinities with *The Marriage of Figaro*; he sent the following comments to the writer:

> *A pompous, fat and elderly suitor favoured by the father has his nose put out of joint by a dashing young lover; could anything be plainer? All your characters are marvellous, drawn very sharply. Do not forget the public should laugh, not smile and grin.*

This request for 'down-to-earth' comedy was resisted by Hofmannsthal, a lyric poet of great sensibility; yet surely, as a young Austrian, he had been impressed with Suppé's *Fatinitza* and its distinctive double travesty role. In the event, the 'elderly suitor' was made to look absurdly comical whilst Strauss ran riot with some of the music.

In *Der Rosenkavalier*, a jest initiated by a young man at an early stage gets out of hand, so touching on other relations and eventually embarrassing all four leading characters. One of the central themes concerns a woman surrendering a glowing, adulterous affair when her 17 year-old lover turns his affections to a girl of his own age. Marie-Therese, the Marschallin (wife of an Austrian Field-Marshal), sings poignantly that *Heute oder Morgen*, today or tomorrow, the boy will desert her, not realising that the time has arrived, precipitated by her own disinterested action.

Strauss' first jest is hidden before curtain rise in the Prelude, having a delayed significance as the action is seen to occur in a bedroom; the whooping horns have always been admired as a feature of Strauss' musical personality, and one respected writer, William Mann, paid unusual tribute to the prelude's intrusiveness:

> *The introduction is so graphic as to leave us in no doubt that this ardent boy, in his inexperience, reaches his climax much too soon . . . and has to resume activity, less inspiringly. . . .*

The lovers are enjoying early morning endearments when a rumpus is heard outside the chamber. Perhaps the Marshal has returned unexpectedly; if so, young Oktavian, Count Rofrano, must be in fear for his life.

The intruder is the Marschallin's distant cousin, Baron Ochs von Lerchenau, whom she dislikes so much that she has not bothered to read his recent letter stating when and why he was calling.

Oktavian could hide until the danger passes, but he prefers to play the fool. Marie-Therese barely has time to recognise a 'loud, stupid voice' quarrelling outside with her servants before Oktavian reappears in drag, calling himself 'Mariandel, a serving maid'. To the accompaniment of the *Rosenkavalier* theme as a light waltz, the farce begins. The 'maid' looks attractive, the more so because Oktavian is played by a mezzo-soprano in a trouser role.

To pointed musical phrasing, Ochs' greeting includes three steps and a bow, a courtly gesture and the least he can get away with. He suffers from many false values, an egoist as oafish as membership of the minor nobility will permit. He intends to gain his cousin's declared support in a projected marriage to the most eligible girl in his world, Sophie Faninal, whose father, he hopes, is in failing health but owns half Vienna.

Herr Faninal lacks nothing but a title and even in the absurdity of mid-18th century society, must also be a prodigious snob to accept as his daughter's suitor a much older, impoverished man lacking finesse.

Ochs is not unusual in regarding young women of the lower classes as fair game, and he takes immediate fancy to Mariandel, easily being distracted from the main purpose of his visit.

It was the refined custom in Austria that an honoured suitor should appoint a presentable young nobleman to act as go-between, formally offering in token a silver rose to his intended: a rose-bearer, a *Rosenkavalier*, whose motif has comprised the first seven notes, youthfully assertive, of that orchestral prelude. Ochs requests the Marschallin to propose a bearer and she, irritated by Oktavian's idiotic behaviour, selects him in revenge for the task. To allow for resemblances between Mariandel and Oktavian to be observed later, she tells Ochs that the Rosenkavalier shall be a Count Rofrano, half-brother to the illegitimate Mariandel. This amuses Ochs because he has always boasted that his valet in attendance, Leopold, is his own son.

In the custom of the times – the date is 1745 – the Marschallin graciously conducts her morning levée in the presence of diverse visitors of less than courtly status, including refined beggars, milliners, gossip-mongers, parrots, puppies, monkeys and dwarfs, any one of whom may be worthy of Strauss' musical attention. This scene of visitors with something to gain is introduced, as several tradeswomen rush in, by an exquisite pastiche of 18th century music, including a florid Italianate aria to be sung by a professional singer.

Ochs is engrossed in drawing-up a marriage contract with the assistance of his cousin's lawyer and treats the assembly with complete disregard, greedily disputing legal details until his persistent shouting reduces the singer to enraged silence.

Two intriguers, on the make, offer to keep a watch on the Baron's fiancée, then Leopold fetches the box containing the silver rose. The Marschallin is left to shrug-off her moral indignation about this betrothal before indulging in a poignant leave-taking with Oktavian, now restored to his fine uniform. The fear, the certainty, that one day Oktavian will desert her is expressed in an impassioned Resignation motif prominent through the first act and returning at a critical moment near the end of the opera.

A charming trap for two lovers has been set for the second act, and a very different one, for Baron Ochs, will emerge in the third.

■ ■ ■

The presentation of the silver rose is one of the most radiant scenes in 20th century opera, Oktavian and Sophie experiencing love-at-first-sight and to ecstatic orchestral sounds. At this unscheduled event, eyebrows are raised among the women attendants, but Sophie's dream is not disturbed until she has first sight of her intended fiancé. His manners make her instantly feel she is household chattel.

For him, much more intriguing is the perceived resemblance of Oktavian to Mariandel. His enjoyment of Marie-Therese's illegitimacy fabrication induces him to joke about rakish fathers with the mystified Count Rofrano. When Ochs approvingly fingers Sophie's flesh, Faninal is assured that his alliance with a branch of the Austrian nobility is now secured.

Every sexual innuendo alienates the girl further, pushing Oktavian to the brink of intervention. Promising Sophie a night of incomparable pleasure, Ochs bursts into the opera's most eloquent waltz melody, opulent in the Viennese style, and thought to derive from Josef Strauss' *Dynamiden Waltz*.[1] To the opening words, *Mit mir* (with me), it is one of the three major theme-songs of the opera:

With me, no night will be too long for you.

Having verified nothing but the girl's biological suitability, he rushes off to complete the overriding financial arrangements, but not before making a comradely gesture towards Oktavian. With the *bonhomie* of two aristocrats slumming in a bourgeois household, he asks the young man to perform an agreeable favour and 'break the girl in', as he does not want her as a virgin.

Alone with Sophie, Oktavian confirms her abhorrence of Baron Lerchenau, whose drunken retainers set about the

female menials. Oktavian draws his sword, then uses it when
Sophie is pressed to sign the marriage document. This
becomes farcical because Ochs scarcely knows how to handle
a sword, screaming 'murder' when Oktavian pricks him.
Faninal is incensed by this youthful rebellion, and fears above
all the ridicule of Viennese society:

> *You'll marry him and if he bleeds to death, you'll marry his
> corpse.*

The options threatened are a convent or prison.

Oktavian eventually withdraws, but the better to jump back;
first to devise a stratagem which will expose Ochs and finally
end Faninal's blind adulation for anyone with a title.

Ochs meanwhile is enjoying the sympathy elicited whilst
being bandaged; when creating this scene,[2] Strauss reminded
Hofmannsthal of the comparison with the *mondo ladro* scene
in Verdi's *Falstaff*:

> *I picture the scene of the Baron after Faninal's exit, similarly the
> Baron on the sofa, the surgeon attending him, the mute servants
> lined up behind the couch and the Baron talking in snatches, in
> turn boastful and sorry for himself, always interrupted by orchestral
> interludes.*

Ochs admits a masochistic admiration for the passionate
young man who has wounded him; the resistance of the
young couple he finds stimulating, a relief from the boredom
of living with underlings. As with Falstaff, a few drinks bring a
euphoric mood caught by music which is suave and relaxed.
With confidence returning, he hums the *Mit mir* phrase, just
as Annina, one of the two schemers now having joined the
opposition, appears bearing a note for him. Accompanied by
a lilting waltz variant of the seven-note motif, she reads out
the contents:

> *Honoured Kavalier, I'm free tomorrow evening. I liked you from the
> start but was shy in front of Milady 'cos I'm so young. In case you
> forgot my name, it's Mariandel, chambermaid in love. I await your
> answer.*

Ochs is susceptible to this turn-around, and seizing the four
last words, sings them in an uncouth Viennese accent, ironically to the *Rosenkavalier* motif. A new, triumphant waltz
theme appears, then whilst Annina spits venom behind his

back, the bandage falls away as Ochs preens himself to a lush recapitulation of the *Mit mir* waltz, and the curtain falls on probably the most sustained deep note in opera.

■ ■ ■

The third act opens with bustling, conspiratorial sounds from the orchestra and on-stage, Mariandel adjusts her dress whilst Annina and her partner put the finishing touches to an entrapment scenario. A sequence of waltzes including several not yet heard lift the gloom from the tavern scene of assignation.

Mariandel's task is to divert the Baron but delay any seduction attempts until the essential witnesses are in place. She has to affect several poses, shyness, giggling, maudlin drunkenness, each one bearing a distinct waltz melody; one of these is derived from a leading motif, and matches the words *Nein, nein*.

In private, Ochs lacks assertiveness, and when most vulnerable, he may seem pathetic, even likeably humorous, one who would escape from flummery and pretence if he could find just one woman who both pleased and loved him.

Just as he removes his wig, and relaxes, freakish characters begin to appear at windows or from trap-doors and he shreiks with fright.

The trap has been sprung too soon because police arrive before the conspirators can summon Faninal, though Ochs' desperate attempt to pass Mariandel off as his fiancée will compromise him further. A disguised Annina and several children claim to be his deserted family and two 'debt collectors' arrive to harass him further.

Leopold standing guard has sensed danger and summoned the one person with the authority to put matters right at a gesture. So that the Marschallin drops into a scene of which she is not *au fait*, being versed in love intrigues, she has to face an unsubtle joke when it is turning sour. Yet she instantly asserts herself, mistress of the moment:

> *This is a Venetian masquerade, nothing more; I'd not like you to seduce my Mariandel. Now I'm rather prejudiced against men, in general, of course.*

Superb dramatic irony. The Marschallin has fathomed an absurd situation and the least embarrassing option for Ochs is to get out straightaway. A sense of humour, especially about sexual liaisons, helps him out. To a quizzical wood-wind version of the Resignation motif, he edges towards the truth:

The Field Marshal – Oktavian – Mariandel – the Marschallin – Oktavian. . . . But what am I to think of this delicious matter?

he asks, now hoping to be paid for his silence, but she gives him the unchallengable answer:

I expect you, as a gentleman, to think absolutely nothing.

The truth is out, and at once sealed up again. Ochs is hammered further as the multitude return, spectres which harass him once more to whooping sounds from the orchestra; he calls to Leopold, then sweeps out, bringing the episode to a grand-stand choral finale.

Sophie returns knowing that her father will reject Ochs, whom she now rebukes with spirit; but at a distance, she overhears sufficient to sense a liaison between Oktavian and Marie-Therese. She is shattered: the chief victim of this 'masquerade' is herself. To a dejected minor key version of the *Rosenkavalier* theme, she can only comment *Es ist vorbei* (It's all over), and the Marschallin, as in a dream, repeats the words.

In this moment of clarity, emotions snap, the comedy is finished, but not the dream. She feels the realisation of her worst fears, but in generosity will recommend to Faninal the betrothal of the young couple. Sophie in gratitude suddenly finds her emotions released in girlish effusion, only to be told:

Don't talk too much. You're pretty enough.

The love triangle is made explicit in a résumé of the motifs and the conflicting emotions of the play, an incomparable trio of two sopranos and one mezzo. The Marschallin walks away in great dignity, Oktavian and Sophie remaining for a blissful duet in the style of Mozart which brings the opera to an end.

■ ■ ■

Rosenkavalier is recognised as containing three of the greatest character roles in the operatic repertoire; the woman of supreme poise and sensibility, a *buffo* comic of outsize stature and one of the most glamorous 'principal boy' roles. It might be regarded as a hybrid, music drama and Viennese musical, powerfully diverse in expression, producing tears both of laughter and sadness.

Strauss' many pronouncements on operetta are ambivalent. The genre was part of his essential south German culture, and he joked that he could compose the greatest of all to outshine the acknowledged Viennese masters. It is curious that he may have felt competitive or even hostile towards Franz Lehár, his almost exact contemporary, despite their successes, though total, being so divergent. Lehár was the greatest operetta composer of his generation.

Strauss at times expressed disapproval of Lehár's 'sentimentality'. One can only speculate on how far this would have surfaced if Lehár had accepted an earlier option to compose *Der Rosenkavalier.*

15 *Classical Burlesque: Ariadne*

Wherever rich fools exist, there are those ready to relieve them of their wealth. This theme is common to important comedies by Molière, including *Le Bourgeois Gentilhomme*. Monsieur Jourdain suffers one of the best-remembered confidence tricks in world comedy, at the hands of an impoverished parasite, Dorante. Jourdain's only helpful asset is a likeable family with sufficient of the common sense which he lacks; but great wealth has exposed his vanity and a pathetic desire to be admired as a cultivated gentleman (*gentilhomme* meaning nobleman in French).

He is led to believe that education can be acquired as effectively as a course of treatment at the doctor's or the hairdresser's: from the moment a self-styled philosopher teaches him that for the whole of his life he has been speaking prose, he believes that cultural vistas are open to him. Trying to ape courtly habits, Jourdain imagines he could enjoy a secret liaison with a fine lady, but lack of poise and gallantry prevent him making a direct approach. Dorante offers to act as go-between, dangling the prospect of success with one such person, who happens to be the object of his own attentions and is not to be made aware of Jourdain's interest. He is easily talked into giving a splendid banquet to which she will be invited along with Dorante whose presence will, as she is to understand, enhance the host's status.

If he had lived at least one generation later, Richard Strauss could have been an incomparable writer of film music; here he composes a 17th century pastiche, close to the style of Lully who had provided the music for the original production. The inept manner in which Jourdain addresses himself to lessons with music and dancing masters became perfect material for Strauss: he illustrates with music the gaucheness of his fencing, and the grand banquet is accompanied by esoteric allusions, such as an extract from his *Don Quixote* when the lamb is served and Wagner's Rhine motif for the fish.

A frequent 17th century court entertainment had been the

comedy-with-ballet, and Molière provided a farcical ending to light this up. Jourdain was persuaded to be enrolled as a *Mamamouchi*, an improbable honour bestowed at the highest level by representatives of the Turkish Sultan; even members of Jourdain's family exasperated by his pretentious and spendthrift ways connive in this charade. There is a colourful parade with song and dance directed by bogus Turks.

Jourdain, intoxicated by these events, wearing expensive 'Turkish' dress and mouthing the ceremonial gibberish he has been taught, is eventually alone with the woman just long enough to betray that the banquet was intended to win her affections. More dupe than accomplice, and embarrassed by two unwanted suitors, she escapes on Dorante's arm from the one who is the bigger fool.

Librettist Hofmannsthal intended to preserve the Molière spirit, but reduced the text to two acts, eliminating a sub-plot with love interest, but retaining all the characters who contribute to Jourdain's humiliation. He would write two distinct items as a final show with Strauss contributing a full score and Jourdain's entourage commenting on the action. The rationale was that the Composer in the play has prepared a divertissement which unites two lovers and this should follow the banquet, whilst a harlequinade would complete the entertainment. Jourdain's fatuous proposal, to prevent his being bored, was that the separate parts should occur side-by-side, lovers and clowns thrown together.

The classical element was to be taken from legend, as had been the norm in the early operas of the 17th and 18th centuries: Ariadne's being deserted on a desert island by Duke Theseus after she had rescued him in an act of love from the Minotaur. The arbitrary joining of the parts was to provide dramatic contrast between the high-minded, god-like Ariadne and a pantomime character, Zerbinetta, who collects real lovers as comfortably as false compliments.

The finished product, entitled *Der Bürger als Edelmann* (The bourgeois with noble pretentions), was worked out through correspondence between the two collaborators living far apart, with Strauss pulling his sceptical partner along the path of burlesque. The form it took was, for a 20th century audience, unfamiliar; leading German-speaking cities saw it from 1912, but the author was quick to comment that even under

Max Reinhardt, it was not proving an overwhelming success.
He thought that the (excellent) music held-up the action
which most people wanted in Molière; it was a unique, 'combined work of art', neither precisely drama nor opera, and
needing a connoisseur audience which it allegedly did not
have in such places as Berlin.

Strauss was a relatively easy man to work with, constructive
in the face of criticism, and he warmed to the notion of
replacing the Molière play with a staged Prologue preceding
a much elaborated *Ariadne*, an opera innovative in form,
some two hours long; *Ariadne on Naxos*. Yet by this time, the
collaborators were working on what was to prove their most
conceptually difficult project, *The Woman without a Shadow*;
that Strauss should so willingly take on a second task is one of
the curiosities of their well-documented correspondence.

Ariadne's suffering had been used for at least 40 known
operas, and Strauss found it interesting because the theme
was familiar enough to be subjected to sophisticated burlesque; and he was enchanted by the personality of
Zerbinetta. Work on these themes would provide welcome
relaxation to a man with an exceptional appetite for composing.

Jourdain's replacement was to be a Viennese patron, and a
fictitious Composer would become the central character in
the first part, the new Prologue. His composition was to be
the augmented divertissement about Ariadne, and he is
thrown into deep confusion when the patron decides that,
noble though the heroine's sufferings are, they might
become tiresome for the audience; so the romance is to be
played alongside a harlequinade with music.

The duality is maintained throughout: watched over by
three nymphs resembling Wagner's Rhine Maidens, who sing
in warm, engulfing waves of song, Ariadne at first silently
contemplates love and death on the island of Naxos. Zerbinetta sings of the pleasures of life and discovering fresh lovers
whilst accepting the homage of four subservient males. It is
however morally and aesthetically desirable that Ariadne is
the one to achieve real fulfilment.

The Prologue offers turbulent examples of the conflicting
tensions back-stage which could accompany last-minute preparations for any première, with Strauss composing to

knock-about humour. He knew Mozart's excellent *Impresario*, a short musical farce on this theme, and the inspiration of other Mozart operas is apparent, such as a classical serenity in much of Ariadne's singing.

The prima donna and lead tenor, who play Ariadne and her future lover, Bacchus, evidently consider themselves more important than the work, the ensemble, or than one another. They have to be given conflicting promises of their dominant roles, along with the soubrette who arrives as the leader of the harlequinade, who, five in number, are like a barbarian invasion; apart from being a naturally discordant element, their lack of prepared script or music could be disastrous. Yet in the age of aristocratic patrons, there were always servants at hand to make a command triumph over practicalities; the pretty singer who is to play Zerbinetta, one is assured, is a mistress of improvisation, a three-ringed circus. So it turns out.

The Composer is dedicated to the realisation of Ariadne's death, transfiguration and eternal unity with Bacchus, and sings some of these motifs. Zerbinetta overhears this soliloquy, then starts to ingratiate herself into a major role by playing on the young Composer's susceptibilities. She offers to bring some 'common sense' to bear on the plot so that the audience will be amused.

Her intimate scene with him is musically and dramatically superb, she posing as one who smiles only on the outside, a lonely comédienne whose inner life is tragic. There follows a characteristic Straussian 'recognition' scene of great tenderness, except that the Composer is probably seeing what does not exist, in his infatuation for the girl whose flirtations just conceal her shallow nature. She will not seduce him, but exercise a hypnotic spell, then slip away. The impressionable young man is fired-up; music is the most sacred of arts, the librettist can achieve wonders and life is beautiful for those with courage. Yet when Zerbinetta returns with her crew, he quickly perceives that she is as vulgar as the rest.

To a dismissive harpsichord flourish, the spell is broken, and the back-stage conflicts once more press upon the Composer. His role, always intended for soprano or mezzo, is poignant: idealistic but in the unforeseeable conditions disoriented, in the last moments before the curtain rises he attempts to distance himself from the company in rage at the desecration of his art. He finally kicks the text around destructively.

The clowns are free to comment upon the opening scene, with its concentration on the deserted heroine; they conclude that Ariadne is losing her mind and can only be healed by their style of music-making. This is crude but lusty though Zerbinetta adds some beautiful melody. She attempts, after Ariadne's impassioned monologue, to empathise about men's faithlessness, but without effect. Soon left alone, Zerbinetta is free to show her real face, indulging in one of Strauss' most astonishing arias, perhaps in his intent the most important of the opera. To the theme of the exquisite emotions which accompany every fresh love affair:

> *God, if you wanted women to resist men, why did you make them all so different?*

she tones-up with a brief catalogue of her lovers' names and some gentle warbling before setting-off in rising coloratura style until at half-stage, to a comment which ironically mirrors Ariadne's unrealised fate, she experiences a brief ecstatic release:

> *Each man came like a god and transported me. . . .*

The aria becomes more tender before continuing its rise, words no longer significant, in a sequence of theatrical climaxes which appear not to have an ending. When Zerbinetta finally comes to rest:

> *Each man came like a god and made me speechless. . . .*

the repetition of this final word, essentially one syllable, in German *stumm*, adds humour to a gratifying cadence. She falls flat on her back, motionless, which by chance can be effectively prolonged because the song is always followed by lengthy applause.

This is in part a parody of the excessively florid Italianate aria which during the 18th century had become dominant: except that this one is meaningful and requires skills beyond singing, such as miming. Strauss would have been thinking of Mozart's (sexual) *Catalogue song* from *Don Giovanni*, though the similarity lies only in the words. There is a widely known reference to this slice of coloratura virtuosity as the 'Grand

National of opera', with its fearsome difficulties for a high soprano which preclude most soubrettes with appropriate youth, looks and acting skills from considering it. Strauss eventually had to agree to shortened or simplified versions.

Zerbinetta is now joined by her four comic-grotesque companions, and she determines the following order of play with the clowning observation that jealousy makes a man give way and dance. To thumping waltz rhythms which are outrageously compelling, a jealousy charade is to follow. She 'hides' with Harlequin, who is the least repellent of the men, to dissolve into rapturous song, recalling phrases from her earlier solo:

> *Never a whim, always a necessity. . . .*
> *The heart understands itself so little. . . .*

whilst the other three imitate the frustrated, enraged postures of love's victims.

Hofmannsthal was to permit no comic digressions from the idyllic final scene in which the nymphs lead up in euphonious narrative to the arrival on the island of the youthful god, Bacchus. There is instant love between him and Ariadne and their deification brings forth some of Strauss' most ravishing melodies. His plan for Zerbinetta to comment on this scene was eventually reduced, but she adds confidingly, as if describing a fairy tale, 'we surrender, *stumm, stumm.*'

Though writer and composer lengthily debated where and how the balance between the epic and comic would be struck, the overall impact is that of a work of high art. Zerbinetta is not dominant, the other protagonists having their musical jewels: Ariadne an almost classic style of lamentation, Bacchus a rich, commanding tenor role, the nymphs excited narrative and a most tender Berceuse. The Composer holds the stage from the start, when he conceives his splendid Venus theme, and suffers fluctuating emotions throughout the first act.

The opera reflects many of the fine qualities of *Der Rosenkavalier*, with its combination of ecstacy, sadness and farce; it converts some of those expressive powers into a chamber opera, with a small orchestra and no chorus. It may be judged as an after-thought to the earlier opera, but an inspired one, and an idiosyncratic mingling of classical and popular music styles.

With Hofmannsthal, Strauss conceived two later works with very light-hearted scenarios. The first was based on a variant of the Menelaus theme, in which the Helen who eloped with Paris to Troy was a fraud, whilst the faithful wife had been spirited off to Egypt 'for the duration'. Perhaps unfortunately, the libretto was more serious, if not obscure, than Strauss could have wished; the finished product, *The Egyptian Helen*, has not been well understood or often performed, being the last of Strauss' operas to reach Britain finally as late as 1997.

Arabella is a domestic comedy in which the heroine's marriage hopes are almost ruined when an unwanted suitor imagines he is spending the night with her, of necessity in the dark; the family honour is saved when Arabella's younger sister confesses to having crept into Arabella's bed. Hofmannsthal's stage play has been greatly admired, and despite an exuberant carnival scene, the music generally has an intensity which takes it far from operetta.

So *Ariadne* stands as Strauss' best-loved, probably greatest light opera, and he explained this in a cool self-assessment:

> *What I've written with my left hand has turned out well ... I always want too much and sometimes spoil it ... this has not happened with Ariadne.*

The apparent ease with which here Strauss created idyllic sound has sometimes become a stick to beat him with; would he be taking an easier path towards mere note-spinning in some of his later operas? Had he passed beyond his full vigour, and beyond what had made him unique? A more general view is that *Ariadne* is one of the peaks in his creativity, but not the final one.

16   *Time-Travel and Leos Janáček*

Moravian composer, Leos Janáček (1844–1928) was influenced by his native music and speech rhythms, which suit the naturalistic style of his operas, of which seven have in recent years been performed in London. He moved away from traditional romantic themes, but only one of these is entirely satirical. *Mr Brouček's Excursions* is based on Svatopluk Čech's writings (1888) which used time-travel humorously, in the company of his invention, Mr Brouček, which means 'little beetle' and rhymes with what we spell Czech.

He is to typify one kind of Prague citizen, interested in beer, food and his problems as a landlord, spending his leisure mostly at a famous inn where Čech once courted the innkeeper's daughter. Thoroughly unimaginative, Brouček is uncomfortable with the arty clientèle, and still more unsuited to space travel. His first trip will be to the moon, whose most interesting function in literature has been satirical. Here, the inhabitants are seen to be aesthetes pursuing trendy but insubstantial forms of artistic expression.

This *Excursion* existed as a short opera by 1909 and might have remained intact if the Great War (1914–18) had not intervened to sharpen Janáček's perspective, especially about the immediate fate of the provinces of Bohemia and Moravia in the Austrian half of the Habsburg Empire. Janáček lived in a district with a large Austrian population, and nationalist sentiments urged him to add to the opera a second *Excursion* which would support patriotic feelings among the Slavs of what are now called the Czech lands.

In the 15th century, these provinces had constituted the Kingdom of Bohemia, linked to the Holy Roman Empire. Its Emperor and the Holy Church had regarded the religious reformers as subversive, and in 1415 their leader, Jan Hus, was burnt as a heretic. The centre of Hussite resistance was at Tabor, and in 1520 they had their historic victory over the Emperor's 'Catholic' army which the Pope had designated a

crusade. The militancy of those Hussite Czechs whom Brouček blunders into is an example to be followed in 1917–18 to
establish the independent state of Czechoslovakia; Janáček
dedicated the completed opera to the Republic's first Presi-
dent, Thomas Masaryk.

The locality for Brouček's departure is the Vikarka inn,
near St Vitus' Cathedral, Prague, on a fresh night with a full
moon. Čech often drank there, with other writers and artists
who late in the evening toast the landlord, Mr Würfl. A
trifling lovers' quarrel induces Mazal, a poverty-stricken
young artist, to promise jewels for his girl-friend, Malinka.
This and other theatrical postures includes her making an
absurd threat to marry his landlord, Mr Brouček.

The older man, drunk or sober, is incapable of relating
socially, which everyone realises is because he lives 'on the
moon'. The pot boy rushes-up to hand him the string of
sausages he has left behind, and in a drunken stupor, Brouček then imagines a lunar exile where he could escape from
taxes, hard-up tenants and other impediments to his happiness.

As the lovers indulge in the sweet tones of reconciliation, a
heavenly violin theme against the night sky gives hope of
ecstatic happenings. The Prague sky-line vanishes as some
part of Brouček takes off, to be promptly confronted on a
lunar landscape by a weird creature dismounting from a
Pegasus. He takes this to be his artist-lodger in disguise to
avoid paying rent. Yet he cannot shake off this apparition
which describes itself as a distinguished moon poet and is
keen to elicit praise for its verses and harp-playing; Brouček
wants neither, responds insensitively and is denounced as a
vulgarian in odd clothing.

Worst of all, he presumes to eat a sausage, admitted to
contain animal flesh, and is condemned as a cannibal.

The poet's girl friend, Etheria, is said to be an incomparable beauty but in Brouček's eyes a gossamer Malinka. She first
likens him to Medusa the Gorgon, but horrid fascination
quickly turns to infatuation. Her father wisely tries to keep
her ensnared in a butterfly net, but when he recites a thesis on
aethetics which sounds to earth-dwellers like a comic patter-
song, she escapes, snatching the earth-man to elope
Walkyrie-like on Pegasus.

She takes refuge at the splendid Temple of All Knowledge where Mr Würfl's voice is heard explaining that though no genuine art-lover, he has been promoted to academy director with a fancy title. There is more high-flown versification, and some listeners even sympathise with Brouček's boredom, especially as it is oddly assumed that he is a vastly superior earth poet. When he calls for beer, he is offered flowers which he is urged to smell for sustenance and intoxication.

The moon-dwellers never enjoy physical contact, and are scandalised by Brouček's praise of sexual intimacy; for them, babics arrive by the spiritual equivalent of a stork. Etheria who is being chased once more by her father, escapes capture and expresses a deep passion for Broučck. Convinced he is surrounded by lunatics of all kinds, he spits sausages at Etheria who disintegrates into a large cobweb; so at the height of the musical festivities he flies off on Pegasus, and these glorious events proceed the better for his absence, the whole assembly in song as they fade into the distance.

In Prague, they are soon laughing about the anti-hero carried home in a box, but the episode is not too undignified to prevent him boasting later of his unique moon visit. The following evening there is a discussion about the existence of sinister underground passages from the castle under the River Vltava. Brouček argues not unreasonably that many kings kept such secrets which historians have not yet exposed, but Würfl ridicules the notion with a shot on target:

You're a credulous fellow, what with your recent excursion. . . .

Brouček, suddenly alone, finds himself in a cellar whence he is propelled through an opening door into King Wenceslas IV's Treasure Chamber. Fearful that he is about to plumb the depths as he has once toured the heavens, he makes for an exit into the old Town Square. Before reaching it, he is confronted by the Poet, Čech, who feels guilty on recalling the heroes of the Battle of Vitkov Hill (the White Mountain.) He apologises for the untimely satirical edge of his verses, but this is the literary style which most suits himself and his contemporaries who have lost their idealism. He hopes a new generation of writers will arise to articulate a renewed faith and do justice to the heroic past.

It is morning as Brouček surveys a just recognisable Square

with dismay, complaining at the lack of civic amenities. One of the characters in fancy dress, a self-styled councillor, takes this as a reproach and approaching Brouček, calls him a 'varlet'. When the official takes the visitor's strange 1888 dialect as evidence that he comes from another Slavonic country, the indignant Brouček responds by accusing him of talking like a pedlar. He is told that this is the year AD 1420, the scene an embattled Prague, and in no time, he is denounced by the mob as a spy for the insurgent 'crusader' prince, Sigismund.

His explanation, that he speaks bad Czech as a result of years living in Turkey, is accepted by a friendly citizen who offers him hospitality in return for his being recruited to the militant cause. Brouček becomes mindlessly involved in religious politics; when he suggests that clerical vestments are the norm, he offends the Hussites because he sounds like a Papist. He cannot see the danger he is walking into, and to the locals, he makes himself ridiculous by asserting that these events occurred in the distant past, Sigismund's army having been defeated by the Hussites under their leader Zizka at Vitkov Hill.

Armed and forced into battle, on encountering the Catholics, Brouček throws away his weapon and pleads for mercy, a treasonable action once the citizens are victorious. When picked up by Taborite warriors, he spins a tale of valour that would have graced Falstaff. Unaware that he is dealing with the most uncompromising faction among the Hussites, he commits the ultimate blunder of saying he has fought alongside the Taborites' leader, Zizka. So he is taken for trial and condemned to death and a quick return to Satan.

Since his liking for beer is already known, the fitting end is that he be burnt in a barrel. Yet the only flame applied is a candle held by his landlord, when he is found groaning over the expected torture. The opera ends with his account of how he has just defeated the crusaders and saved his native Prague.

Inept in any situation outside the utterly familiar, Brouček is a neurotic traveller, so never bursts into sweet melody. Though caught in streams of recitative, his reactions are always negative. He imagines the main accusers in 1420 are his housekeeper (in the form of a woman whom he calls a witch) and Mazel (pretending to be a Hussite fighter). Mazel had talked of his love for waltzing, and it is the waltz which dominates music fashions on the moon, where it is performed in astounding variations of tempo.

Etheria's perverse desire for Brouček provokes a post-romantic trio with two males out of countenance, but the tone is subtly Wagnerian. The Medusa allusion was topical as Janáček's opera was conceived when Richard Strauss in *Salome* and *Elektra* was pulling 'modern' music drama towards the neurotic and the grotesque, with the repellent 'heroines' lusting for blood. Etheria, in contrast, offers Brouček a variety of love, elsewhere known as Platonic, and sings beautifully, except for an excess of figurative language which lives among banalities:

> *Your look has stopped my heart from beating*
> *and yet my heart responds with a choral.*
> *And on my lips I feel the kiss of muses,*
> *and like a frightened sea, my spirit fathoms*
> *your face's features and seeks to find your heart,*
> *like that courageous mountain dweller*
> *who amid the rocks looks for the amethyst.*

The *Moon Excursion* originally stood alone, a satire on the pretentiousness of certain writers, with an epilogue which was later suppressed. Further use of Čech's ideas had met with difficulties, especially finding the ideal librettists for the second *Excursion* though many were consulted. The statement by the Poet may now be omitted in some productions, but in the late 19th century and after, Czech nationalism had asserted itself with some success in cultural matters, operating legitimately within the Bohemian constitution.

The moon anthem is a joke, but the Hussite songs are strongly emotive, whilst women's voices express the tragic aspects of war, especially the death of Brouček's host in battle. The men tend towards declamatory expression, and there are several uplifting choral passages where faith is underlined by added passion in the orchestra. The traditional Hussite hymn, heard in the distance, signifies the ongoing battle at Vitkov Hill.

The Hussite reformers demanded an end to corrupt practices within the Church governed from Rome, but the purifiers of history have often been narrowly sectarian, and regard any opposition as the work of Satan. There is expressed some disagreement among the Praguers about the role of their Taborite allies, the age-old conflict between moderates or compromisers and 'men of principle' or fanatics

A new, brief epilogue recalls some of the most powerful secular music for the Hussite warriors. The first is folksy and to our ears attractively Scottish, and an exuberant fanfare incites Brouček to boast about fighting alongside Zizka. Yet his childlike relief at reaching the safety of home, accompanied by music for a fairy tale, comes nearest to winning sympathy.

Janáček wrote most of his own libretti, and intended this work to have Expressionist features, a movement fashionable in the early decades of the 20th century. This is shown in the use of stereotypes, cartoon characters and fanciful or absurd names. No female would be called Malinka because it is the common Czech word for a young girl.

Expressionism obviates the need for any kind of realism, and the staging of these two operas in one needs the most imaginative treatment if it is not to fall into anti-climax. The opening gives prominence to Prague's historically preserved skyline against a cramped street-scene; in contrast the first lunar expanse can be as desolate as any trendy producer could desire. The 1938 Brno production took a bold step (at that time) of inserting a transparent platform so that the moon-dwellers appeared to be walking on air. These creatures tend so far towards exaggeration that any modern presentation of their arts and music festival should vie in hyperbole with the greatest media excesses likely to be endured during the 21st century. The second *Excursion* is less problematic for an art form which has specialised visually for nearly two centuries in medieval romance, but the great battle must be given dramatic immediacy, the most poignant moments in the whole opera.

17 A Hungarian Fantasy

For more than two centuries, Hungary had close political and cultural links with neighbouring Austria. A complex relation was vexed through the development of nationalism during the 19th century, and also produced much creative tension. Hungary's music would make a very big impact in Europe, and Zoltan Kodaly (1882–1967) was to achieve fame internationally as composer and pioneer of teaching methods.

As a young man, dedication to the music of his country led to his compiling invaluable folk archives by notating the performances of local musicians who had memories of rural Hungary back into the previous century. Subjecting them to this new form of research was a very difficult though rewarding task: his nation's folk music was to become the inspiration for his own compositions.

Expelled after the 1914–18 war, Hungary's King[1] had been for centuries the Habsburg ruler, resident in Vienna, which for Kodaly symbolised undesirable foreign influences. After the war, he looked back on an era, commenting on the past Austro-Hungarian relationship, expressed in terms of broad humour rather than political invective.

This was in one of his most important and attractive works, *Hary Janos (1926)*, part play and part opera. In the political uncertainties of the time, the strong national feeling made its appearance a sensation far beyond musical circles.

Of a total of 30 musical numbers, most are of songs Kodaly had collected. Prominent is an exciting melody by the gipsy Bihary, whose compositions had achieved great popularity, as far as the more cosmopolitan society of hotels and cafes outside Hungary.[2] *Hary Janos* is a work of great originality with powerful emotive appeal alongside a sequence of comic stories.

These are an old soldier's fabrications by Hary, a Hungarian patriot who had lived to become legend, especially to small boys. Kodaly did not impose any modern or rebellious notions on a man, real or legendary, who would not have understood Napoleon's policy of liberating Europe from feudalism. Yet Hary had lived under such a system, a peasant tied to the land except when drafted into military service. For him, the Habsburg Empire may have represented a kind of stability against marauding war-lords, and also a Christian outpost against the Turkish hordes that had once occupied most of Hungary.

In the bare-faced lies about his travels and duties in military service for the Emperor, he intended no ridicule or disloyalty. He just loved entertaining with wild descriptions of how he defeated Napoleon, no less funny if his audience knew that the French army without Napoleon won its only battle on Hungarian territory at Győr in 1809. Such picturesque distortions place Hary in the mould of a Münchhausen, Quixote or Falstaff; his adventures occupy the four central scenes of the opera.

Balancing Hary's loyalty to the Emperor and the social order, his intended wife, Örsze (Lizzie), is indifferent to the strange conventions of life outside her small village. She calls upon God to punish those responsible for taking her man away, with one finger pointing at the Emperor. Her funnier moments are unintended: the double-headed eagle, emblem of the Habsburg Monarchy, is for her one more fowl for the pot. But she relaxes to sing a comic song about farmyard animals, which have always had their place in folk music.[3]

The work starts with a musical joke, a full orchestral sneeze to describe a Hungarian response on hearing fanciful stories, but followed by a brooding Prelude before the narration begins.

Far more than England, much of Europe suffered over centuries from invading armies, which is the reason male dancing has a strong military element. This is an important feature of Hungarian folk music and its *verbunkos* derived from recruitment songs is compelling in rhythmic verve, stirring the blood to rash action. Once lured into joining the colours, the soldiers have years to contemplate their fate, the grief and added hardship of their families.

The Hussars' chorus sweeps away all such worries, and its stamping rhythm is one of the central motifs in *Hary Janos*, an incitement to drink and instant enjoyment. The first military scene is on the Galician frontier, a lonely flute plays a theme which symbolises the Hungarian countryside, and the local Ruthenian[4] women sing a wordless chorus. Hary knows that the temperature on the Hungarian side of the border is much warmer than that on the Russian, so by stretching his arm out, good Hungarian wine may be cooled.

The Russian guards are obstructing the journey of Marie-Louise, an Austrian Archduchess recently obliged to marry the victorious Emperor Napoleon Bonaparte. Courteous Janos carries the frontier post temporarily into home territory and the girl proceeds but not before arranging to have this handsome, enterprising sergeant accompany her to Vienna where he is to prove adept with horse-breaking and curing the Emperor's illness.

Hary's men are transferred to the Italian front; they sing of their homeland, then in Hungarian fashion, rush into exhilarating tempo as they summon up the courage for battle. This typifies the slow-fast rhythmic pattern which, stylised, has become world famous as Hungary's most characteristic dance, the csardas.

The battle joined, the Hungarian troops march forward to strident trumpets, withstanding the first cavalry change from the French, continuing to advance into a brief, decisive clash. Four solemn notes announce victory and the enemy are dispersed with a distorted version of the *Marseillaise*, a whining Napoleon grotesquely humiliated. On realising he has been fated to meet the invincible Hary face to face, Napoleon prostrates himself, bemoaning the lesson in military tactics just given by the great Hungarian hero. Then comes a final submission:

> *I do most humbly repent those sins committed by me against His Majesty, the Emperor Francis, and the devastation to his land. I commit myself to pay 50,000 Thalers in one sum. (Cheers) ... Because of my impertinence in attacking Hary Janos of Great Abony, I give my Imperial word I shall behave myself from now on and that there shall be no more complaints by or against me.*

Napoleon limps off into captivity, accompanied by wailing bassoon and the stunned French reaction is caught in a meandering saxophone with notes leaning dejectedly on one another.

Hary has displayed such panache that his own commander-in-chief gladly exchanges rank with him; puffed up with this new authority, but magnaminous in victory, he sums up Napoleon's defeat:

> *It's not your fault; as long as you only had to fight the Germans, the Turks and the Russians, your Grand Army could cope . . . as long as they never met the Hungarian Hussars . . . and now that they have, you want to go home crying to your Mama. It's not your fault; where would you have been able to recruit real Hussars?*

Infatuated with the victor, Marie-Louise visits the camp, a rare chance to live it up, and ordering the gipsy fiddlers to get started. Lizzie's arrival threatens to break up the party; she is angered to find her heroes drinking and dancing, especially with this Princess:

> *Your Highness has gold, diamonds, silver. I have nothing but Hary Janos. He is mine – if you try to take him from me, I'll scratch your eyes out.*

Marie Louise is spoilt, a handful for anyone, and there is much knock-about humour, in the manner of traditional Hungarian light musicals, which often have a 'town versus country' scenario. Hary cannot control his paragon of Hungarian womanhood, nor can he refuse the Austrian girl, who happens to be the French Empress. So in his confusion, he agrees to accompany her to Vienna where the Emperor may resolve matters. She intends to marry him after divorcing the cowardly Napoleon, but by the time they reach Vienna, her plans are well underway.

The polyglot Empire was extraordinary for having among its peoples up to a dozen national languages and countless dialects, and the variety of accents becomes a source of much humour, whilst the Viennese scenes ridicule the artificialities of court life.

'The Viennese Clock' is a movement for percussion, keyboard and woodwinds, with the appeal of a mechanical ballet and child-like symmetry. This and Marie-Louise's two frivolous songs are 'classical' pastiches, affectionately about her pet bird, but with contempt for the current choice of suitors; whilst the courtiers chant an accompaniment of broken phrases, laughable in its servility but musically caressing. The court children sing a banal ditty, and the farcical climax comes with the entry of a collection of archdukes. This is met by a theme suggesting a ragged army on the march. Several Habsburg princes living in the time of Beethoven and Napoleon were in fact skilled musicians, and would not have recognised themselves. The music is presented tongue-in-cheek as the barbarian sound it might have seemed to most Hungarians.

Marie-Louise is after the Pope's authority to divorce and marry the Protestant Hary, with their being permitted to succeed to the Austro-Hungarian throne. Her father announces his decision to make Hary an Archduke, offering his daughter half the kingdom and full executive powers. This provokes Lizzie to the ultimate protest: Austria has exploited Hungary to the full, and now intends to take from her an Emperor.

The hero duly explains the embarrassment in which he has been placed, then puts matters to rights, and graciously declines all honours, asking only for immediate release to his village, and the halving of his military service. The rejected Marie-Louise screams as he tells her to console herself with one of the available royal dukes, but the Emperor concedes, greatly valuing Hary's magnanimity.

He will leave his huge palace for a humble cottage with Lizzie, departing from Vienna after making the most important statement of his life on behalf of all true patriots:

> *The whole of Hungary seems so small from here but it gives the Empire all its wine, its wheat, its peace. May God grant this but save a little for the Hungarians themselves. I shall go home to plough my Emperor's countryside.*

He walks off the stage proudly in his uniform; except for the opening scene, the opera has been a fantasy, and the Napoleonic episode an amusing diversion. A fresh vision of reality brings two emotive themes to represent the people and the continuity of the landscape. First is a soaring Intermezzo, heard also after the victory *en route* to Vienna; composed by Kodaly, it is close in spirit to the Hussars' song on Bihary's melody.

The stage becomes darkened; Hary reappears in his village of Great Abony looking much older, poorly clothed, limping on his crutches, just one of the peasants working from dawn till dusk. Lizzie and other folk are huddling from the cold.

They join in chorus the music which evokes the beloved lands
between the rivers Danube and Tisza.

■ ■ ■

For the 1982 Buxton Festival, a translation of this work made
a strong impact. The music speaks for itself, and as is apparent in a BBC radio hearing, the audience enjoyed the
'nationalist' jokes, responding to the lusty goings-on very
positively.

Kodaly's approach makes a very interesting contrast with
Ferenz Erkel's *Bank Ban* (1861), which in its time was remarkable for introducing the Hungarian idiom, easily identifiable,
into opera, without however displacing the Italian melodic
and formal influence.

Kodaly's biographer, P.M. Young, praises *Hary Janos*' folk-
song arrangements, its freshness and youthfulness; he calls it
worldly-wise and sardonic, beautiful but without sentimentality, companionable but critical.

The orchestral Suite formed from the work has achieved
great popularity outside Hungary. Its six movements have
very striking melodies and are most colourfully scored,[5] the
even-numbered ones causing much amusement in concert
halls.

The Suite does not attempt to show the predominance of
folk music within the whole opera. That element is passionate
and dignified, whereas the cosmopolitan styles at the court
are trivialised and burlesqued. In these ways, Kodaly rein-
forces his essential didactic argument; that Hungarian
musicians should turn away from the foreign models and
influences which had dominated before the 20th century, to
build upon the riches of their native culture. Not only in
Hungary, such nationalist approaches vitalised music-
making, and broke the tradition of students being schooled
primarily in the great European classics, a process guided for
so long from Vienna.

18   *A Wagner Parody*

During World War I, Gustav Holst used to encourage his students to compose parodies, especially when classes had to retire to Morley College's air-raid shelter. For him, they were extensions of his researches into the music of other times and cultures; one of the reasons for the popularity of his *Planets* is that for once, he took opportunities to parody appealing composers of recent times.

As a young man, he had been a Wagner enthusiast, and in his maturity, wrote a sophisticated parody of his operatic style and that of Verdi. *The Perfect Fool* introduces magic, love potions and an absurd figure whose very insensitivity eventually gives him status. The Wagnerian allusions include Wotan, the god disguised in one opera as an earthly wanderer, his daughter, Brünnhilde, whom for disobedience he encased in a protective ring of fire, and her heroic lover, Siegfried.

This is a tale of inadequate characters involved in a relentless sequence of anti-climaxes, and a peasant cunning enough to promote her indolent, half-witted son. Stereotypes take centre ground, with a contest for a Princess involving two self-styled operatic heroes and a Wizard who can't produce even a little black magic on time.

There is a melodramatic orchestral introduction, with the Wizard conjuring the Spirits of Earth and Air to provide a cup filled with the essence of love distilled, whilst the Spirits of Fire shall dwell within it. By boasting how this magic will gain him possession of the Princess, he sets off events which will bring to an end his appalling existence. The listener is a poor Woman whose son has been the subject of a prophecy, that one day the intensity of his gaze will win a bride and kill a foe.

It is said that all who look at the Princess fall in love, so this pathological villain intends to kill at a glance every man he meets. Fortunately, he considers all females witless and beneath contempt, so on meeting this one, he merely demands unquestioning servitude after demonstrating power over her. He orders her to teach him the courtesy necessary for wooing, then he acts out with her the courtship of the Princess. His singing of a 'prize song' is not his best effort because he is saving all his magic for the big day. Like Beckmesser[1] in *The Mastersingers of Nuremberg*, he is absurdly over-confident, promptly blaming the woman:

> *But why are you so stiff? That's the great point of the song and you've missed it. We must go back and do it properly ... You're the worst actress I've ever met: no feeling, no imagination, no sense of style.*

Now he needs her even more so, proposing she should be a surrogate wife (not a romantic figure in opera), and falls asleep confident that she will watch over him like a good fairy. So all she has to do is conceal her son, and steal the potion, replacing it with pure water which she praises in an ode of surprising delicacy. The Fool is duly instructed to drink the potent brew.

The Princess arrives with a splendid cortège, confident this is the day she will choose her husband, who will be the bravest of all, capable of an act no other can achieve. The Wizard offers himself as the first suitor, but he is greeted by the assembled ladies with ridicule, mainly because he is too old and ugly, according to the Princess who does not mince her words.

He is not discouraged because he will be rejuvenated, and starts his serenade which has such a discordant note that the Princess calls for help. Deflated that the drink has not done the trick, the Wizard retires with threats that he will wreak vengeance on the entire community.

The next suitor is an Italian Troubadour who woos the Princess with a melody reminiscent of Arthur Sullivan out of the drinking song from *Traviata*. His attempts to bring gaiety to the scene show that he is just one more boastful suitor. With such posturing, he provokes the Princess to compete against his high notes, but she beats him hands down and with a final flourish of rich coloratura, he is unceremoniously given the push. As prize songs go, the Troubadour's must be the one most rapidly and melodiously seen off.

Italian singing by the 'twenties hardly needed further burlesquing in Britain, but on this occasion the performance of an ineffectual Troubador throws the ponderous Germanic music which follows into amusing contrast. Its heavy orchestral chromaticism descends into appalling gloom, then instead of a youthful tenor voice, a bass, more Wotan than Siegfried, is heard from a self-styled Traveller. In singing of his 'bride to be', he confidently uses familiar Wagnerian phrases, but all to no effect. He then drifts towards *Tristanesque* despair, a theme from Act III no less. Does he enjoy suffering, or is he, like Wotan, too old for the ecstasy of love? Either way, this Princess has no time for niceties and crushes him with a few words: 'Sir, I think we have heard this before.'

The Traveller exits to music from *The Twilight of the Gods*. This is the moment for Wotan to ensure that the Princess sees her son, and in no time at all the cortège is wailing that she has fallen for a beggar. Against this new threat, the suitors protest, drawing encouragement from more Wagner and a snatch of the sexual catalogue from *Don Giovanni*.

Terrified by the news that the Wizard has set fire to the district, the courtiers flee, leaving the Princess to face him, but serenely she sings of her indifference to earthly dangers. Directed by his mother, the Fool's glance is targeted at the Wizard who is consumed by fire. The Fool must be the most inept hero in opera, but the Princess implores his eternal love with some very high operatic notes indeed. He responds with an expressionless 'NO'!!!

This is his unique vocal contribution to the whole text. The mother and the chorus celebrate, repeating time again that he has performed the impossible by not falling in love with the Princess. A single note, on full orchestra, matches the Fool – the final anti-climax.

The Wizard's music, and what represents the magic fire, is rhythmically most inventive, with an intriguing seven beats to the bar section, and it forms the outer movements of a ballet suite, an orchestral tour de force, far better known than the complete opera. The middle section has ethereal music associated with the Princess's search for love.

A royal bride should be the most popular of operatic clichés, but one who neither gets her man nor dies of grief is an outsider. This one is not endowed with immense charm, or seemingly much imagination, but the ironies of the story did not satisfy *The Perfect Fool*'s first audience. They had not expected one which broke so many conventions and just faded out. Was it incomprehensibly 'modern' or just a joke? Holst was no trendy but very committed and consistently adventurous in his choice of themes.

Successful Wagner parodies are scarce and the work is unique; apart from that and the Italian episodes, the rest of the music suggests that this magical realm lies within the British Isles. Considering the English social scene of the 'twenties, an amusing explanation of the plot was offered by musicologist, Sir Donald Tovey, that the Princess represents Opera, and the Fool the British public.

If the work had appeared some fifty years later, it would have been thought in part as an assertion of feminine superiority, an interpretation which would not have displeased the composer.

19   *Shostakovich in Lighter Mood*

As a drama of the human emotions, the symphony has often embraced humour, from the times of Joseph Haydn to those of Gustav Mahler, whose music was greatly admired by Dmitri Shostakovich, who often applied a lighter touch. This was in accord with policies, uniquely in communist countries, that the most talented composers should write 'popular' as well as 'serious' music. Yet his Ninth Symphony was received with official surprise, written in 1945 when other Soviet composers were preparing grandiose works to celebrate the ending of the war; it is appealingly light, in parts skittish.

Many composers have enjoyed writing at least one work in affectionate parody of great composers. Shostakovich's First Piano Concerto (1933) achieves this aim almost throughout starting with the opening phrase from Beethoven's *Appassionata* Sonata, then introducing many more allusions, not always easily identified, from Haydn and Rossini through to Prokofiev and Ravel. The trumpet *obbligato* in its finale is near in spirit to Haydn's Trumpet Concerto, though not the melody which would have been unimaginable in the 18th century.

For comic and other effects, Shostakovich liked to draw on folk and popular tunes, some from foreign cultures, often enhancing their appeal. Some melodies not born for greatness may be promoted, such as the banal 'Jinglebells', which was subjected to a set of variations in songs for the Fool in his incidental music to *King Lear.*

His film music which is coming to public attention abroad in the form of orchestral suites contains much pastiche. Best known is *The Gadfly (1955)*, about an adventurer in the struggle for Italian unification, with ultra-romantic melodies for the love interest, and dance movements in the contrasting styles, restrained and liberated, of the 18th and late 19th centuries. He took familiar themes from Offenbach's music, reworked and set for ironic effect against revolutionary songs in *New Babylon,* a landmark film by Sergei Eisenstein about the 1870–1 civil war in Paris. For *The Unforgettable Year 1919,* he composed a miniature after the manner of Tchaikovsky's piano concertos. That was in 1951, when by chance there had been a vogue in Britain, with a wealth of classic or specially commissioned works for piano and orchestra to increase the impact as incidental film music.

In any period of social revolution, a fresh disrespectful approach to traditional artistic form is to be expected, but works hastily conceived in this spirit are unlikely to survive. Building on an existing culture is the most effective advance, but opera in the Soviet society from the 1920s would no longer seek romantic themes, the cult of the individual, unless seen to be of value to the community. Ballet had for so long been permeated by stories of fantasy and magic, which were after the revolution targets for ridicule. Shostakovich enjoyed attacking obscurities, with which he associated religion in general. Ballet's great cliché, the triumph of good over evil, still had a purpose once it was politically corrected. As a very young man, he gave full rein in a satirical flair, with two ballets on topical subjects composed and performed by 1931.

Bolt is about sabotage of the communist economy by enemy agents, and tells how a team of footballers foils the 'reactionaries'. The composer treats the curious story as farce, but the music is highly inventive and far superior to everything else about the ballet. *The Age of Gold,* in similar propagandist vein, did not receive much attention at the time but had good long-term prospects because of its choreographic potential and the wealth of attractive music which it has been able to incorporate.

It includes a polka, which was Shostakovich's first comic dance movement to become well-known internationally, like nothing heard before in a concert hall. This is performed by a Harlequin figure at the night club, the central locality of the plot, where seemingly trivial melodies are very fashionable.

The workers, who of course rise to heroic status during the story, do not frequent the club, with its 'creeping' style of dance, but move with remarkable athleticism to more traditional sounds. There is the shock appearance of priest, banker and a swashbuckling general, cavorting before all until faced by indignant workers who drive them away with broomsticks.[1]

The athletic young hero has a girl-friend, Rita, who starts to work at the night-club. There she has to perform a dance which could incite men to passion, but her innocence protects her from fear and she is impressed by her dance partner's expertise. He turns out to be the chief villain and undercover gang-leader with a mistress, whose main appeals are an exciting dress and a lascivious style of dancing. She uses these to lure away two men, who are set upon, robbed and murdered.

The hero intends to warn Rita and visits the club where he has some difficulty in speaking to her confidentially because of the tumult of galops and cancans. Elsewhere, they enjoy three *pas de deux*, one for each act, and to music of gentle lyricism.[2]

Meanwhile, the villain will use any foul means to possess the girl. Once she is alarmed, he holds a knife to her throat, forcing her to participate in a sensual dance. To a man who has just killed his mistress because she took a knife to him in jealousy, this is a sadistic ritual which the guests treat as a charade.

The club has some good tunes: a now famous one, with saxophones and a touch of Hawaii, part way between a tango and a fox trot,[3] is danced to suave elegant perfection. There is a distinguished set-piece for the corps de ballet to the American song, 'Tea for Two', sumptuously orchestrated by Shostakovich.

Admiration for a film actor-comedian, Leonid Utiosov, led Shostakovich to write some 'more serious' music than Leningrad's Musical Comedy theatre normally used. The play, *Hypothetically Murdered (1931)*, was a surreal 'circus revue' to be built around Utiosov's stage versatility, and the descriptive requirements made this an enjoyable task for the composer: an actor walking out on his part and being chased around town, military manoeuvres, male and female waiters rushing about, angels sounding ridiculous in a godless heaven, where Mephisto sings a little of what Gounod wrote for him. Russian saints are in evidence, and the Archangel Gabriel's undignified contribution was later to find its way into that First Piano Concerto.

In 1940, Shostakovich was planning a comic opera on Pushkin's tale of *The Priest and his Servant, Balda*, but because of the war, it was cut down in size for concert performance. The outcome is a robust work, folksy with several comic songs.

The Priest is an exploiter of human labour, and takes on Balda wage-free, hoping to discredit him before the expiry of one year when he would have to pay him a lump sum. Devils abound in the community, but behave more reasonably than the Priest who is superstitious. They dance boisterously in the market place without harming the citizens, and symbolically their assault on the church bells cheers up the music. The loyal servant wins the affection of the Priest's family, but is deliberately set an impossible task. He is to visit the under-world, and extract from the devils payment for debt. As in *The Age of Gold*, virtue wins the struggle and the villain is pun-ished.

The burlesque calls for a curious range of sound effects. There are fleeting reminiscences of Mussorgsky and others back to Mozart, imitation of a balalaika band, well-known songs receiving eccentric orchestration: saxophones, wind instruments at the extremes of their range, and the xylophone which is known to favour diabolical rhythms. The pantomime effects are increased with a child's song, a race between a devil and a hare, and the dance for a Russian bear.

One more large-scale work, light and satirical, was to follow some years after the war, with a very different texture, less fully composed: *Moscow-Cheryomushki* of 1959.

• • •

The Lyric, Hammersmith, provides quality entertainment, thanks to municipal enterprise whose subsidies enable the theatre to offer a stable clientèle innovative modern works, British, American and European classics, new and experi-mental theatre adaptations, and occasional small-scale musicals or operas. There are insufficient such institutions, in this author's experience, to be found in London compared with Berlin.

It supported an initiative by Pimlico Opera (1994–5), one of London's progressive societies, to perform this operetta at a time when such works from Eastern Europe are totally unknown in the West. Moscow and other major cities in that subcontinent each designate at least one theatre for musicals which require trained operatic voices, a genre which has always been adequately supported and not left to the vagaries and music vandalism of commercial financing.

Guests came to see a curiosity, then with favourable reviews, more arrived to enjoy and laugh, full houses were achieved and *Moscow-Cheryomushki* (Cherry-Tree Estate) returned the following year for a further season.

The initial attraction was the composer's name, but the music has an uninhibited populist flavour. It was first performed by a Moscow operetta theatre, where today there is still a large repertoire of Viennese and Parisian classics, and popular Russian works. The work when first produced was seen in the spirit of socialist realism, and as a light-hearted comment on the political and economic reforms propagated in the Kruschev (immediate post-Stalin) era.

It displayed the optimism created by the promise of new housing estates and more consumer goods in a Soviet Union which had suffered an annihilating war, and the austerity of the reconstruction years. It deals with the hopes of families and young couples moving into this new estate and taking on two corrupt officials, who are eventually exposed and demoted.

For this Shostakovich used as theme-song a facile, popular waltz 'hit', *Cheryomushki*, which had reflected the new optimistic spirit of those times, along with many of his own melodies adapted to comic verse and presented in compelling dance rhythms.

Any sophisticated adaptation would now make more explicit the satirical aspects of the original and, by chance, exploit the disillusionment, common to Russian and Western societies, with the 'benefits' of high-rise building estates. Pimlico Opera recognised this as a topical theme, with interesting political overtones, and researched it carefully.

The first requirement was an English version adapted musically for this size of venue. Gerald MacBurney, a Russian specialist, scored the work imaginatively for small band, and David Pountney, formerly of ENO, made the first English translation and provided the lyrics. The quality of these contributions formed the basis of a lively success; there was up-dating where desirable, with a text made intelligible to a young Western audience today without destroying the original spirit or sense of period. A young Russian actress was available to sing the lead, Lidochka, and advise on Moscow life and other subtleties to inform the production.

Seven citizens are moving into the Cheryomushki estate including a young married couple, Masha and Sasha, lacking their own flat, and so obliged to live separately. Lusya is an idealistic construction worker who finds romance with Sergei, but his unreliability finds her singing like a dejected Tchaikovsky. His friend Boris is awaiting with immense confidence, to judge from his preposterous 'balalaika' serenade, the arrival of Miss Right.

She is Lidochka, a young intellectual reminiscent of those guides who used to address foreign visitors glowingly about the Soviet Union and its achievements; she is similarly employed in a museum where the visitors sing ambivalently to a march of progress. She has an angular song, almost Gilbertian with its internal rhymes, itemising her book knowledge, but admitting that a 'swot has got a lot to learn', especially about love.

She will share the new flat with her father, Baburov, an eccentric who lives in the past, indifferent to the official world. He interrupts the euphoric proceedings with a pathetic little song about a congenial spot 'just a little stroll from Lenin's tomb', Warm Lane, which has been spared modernisation.

In this London version, he is zany, at the end of an umbrella, which sometimes propels him high up the backdrop. He also visits members of the audience to see if they are being well entertained, creating some local colour with his authentic Russian accent.

The estate manager has fixed it for a rich official, Dreb, and his mistress, Vava, to have a love-nest of two flats, by knocking down a wall, at the expense of the Baburovs. The anti-social couple are presented as appalling sit-com creatures, and their introductory duet brings to the surface resentments of a relation based on mutual exploitation. To his sub-operatic pleading for her love, she responds:

I don't see the passion is worth all the fuss if I have to travel by bus.

Then they reverse roles, his true feelings equally common-place, since he has 'sacrificed marriage for a pair of tits'; the grotesque pleading of the music is lost when handed over to the band for a fierce climax at double speed.

At the height of their arrogance, the two corrupt officials share a confidential ditty:

> *Now life's a smoothly moving groove but only if you're well connected.*
>
> *What's more, it's well to be connected well if you're not already well connected.*
>
> *Who needs the dross when you're the boss and the cream of nomenclature[4]?*
>
> *The party's there to argue the toss and to judge it by occasion the juror.*
>
> *Your connection says that he can fix your life and that's it's all a favour*
>
> *But once he's on your back he sticks like chewing gum that's lost its flavour . . .*

The ironic tail to this patter song is violin-led, an orchestral gem taken from the *Bolt* ballet.[5] Sardonic instrumental sounds accompany the confrontation of officials and residents, a familiar kind of public meeting, noisy and inconclusive.

Some of the finest 1950s Russian 'hits' (including 'Moscow Nights' aka 'Midnight in Moscow') are prominent in a duet with Boris when Lidochka takes off her spectacles and lets her hair down in an electrifying dance, somewhere between a tearaway gopak and jerky rock-and-roll. She can belie her cool exterior, heating up in a moment; so starting as a wistful aria in Borodin's sinuously 'Asian' manner, this *scena* builds up in shock stages to a final exuberant release, the musical highlight of the whole work.

Led by the activist Lidochka, the good residents finally take action, creating a magic garden with a bench which acts as a truth drug. Once the nasty couple are lured to sit there, he admits he is 'on the make' and they no longer hide their mutual dislike.

The original scenario gained from fantasy elements of a kind which the cinema can best realise, and the Pimlico production responded imaginatively. For the ballet, communist ideology is replaced by the ubiquitous hype of capitalist societies: with a '60s-type TV scenario, the company dance to a fatuous commercial advertisement, washing machine and powder, fairy steam and a soap queen. An energetic group of seven does work for a corps de ballet and large chorus, tripping frequently across the stage in comic disguise and giving sharp commentaries on the scenes in the flats where the plots develop.

■ ■ ■

The work appeared in the form of a Russian film, rather like the Ealing comedies of the 1950s, which had people scampering about to some fixed and farcical purpose; but it is also a song-and- dance spectacular, with emphasis on youth, citizens in collective action, and massed gymnastic displays.

The original film[6] opens with a car trip around the beauties of old Moscow, to an orchestral prelude of immense rhythmic vigour. The flat-warming party has a polka which is also idiosyncratic Shostakovich, and the ballet for the magic garden sequence is a send-up of fairyland and *Swan Lake*. Its bland tones in waltz tempo veer towards Viennese *schmaltz*, before giving way to an exuberant finale where the popular songs in Lidochka's duet get a welcome second run. Shostakovich preferred this film version for its scope in exploiting the many facets of an idiosyncratic musical.

20 *Robin Hood: 1862–1997*

The London Players Theatre's annual festive show always celebrates the era when burlesque was the most popular large- scale form of entertainment on the British stage. For 1996–7, the choice was an 1862 extravaganza, *Robin Hood* by F.C. Burnand.

Modern adaptations are radical, increasing the musical interest and often eliminating the static approach which held up the action for the music. In this Robin Hood version, for example, not one but two villains hatch their plot mainly in song, with sinister notes from Beethoven's 5th Symphony in the background. The new lyrics were written by Maurice Browning, and the original music has been largely replaced by popular excerpts from that of Sullivan, Bizet, Massenet, Offenbach, Foster and Saint-Saens, mostly written after 1862, and added to items by Handel, Verdi and others.

The first act takes place outside the castle of Lady Clare who is under siege from numerous creditors, all local tradesmen. They are in vigorous operatic mood, making their demands to the Prelude from *Carmen*, but she asks for time whilst she marries her beauteous daughter off to the well-heeled Norman, Sir Gilbert de Montfalcon. The audience is promptly urged to sympathise with the girl, Maid Marion, who imagines (to the *Dream* song from Massenet's *Manon*) a lover bright of eye and strong of arm, nothing at all like Sir Gilbert.

Meanwhile, her Maid-of-honour is fascinated by Will Scarlett who has arrived in exciting red leather gear, in advance of his master, the Earl of Huntingdon. This causes Lady Clare some Parliamentary confusion:

> *The Earl of Huntingdon? He, I wager,*
> *In that constituency must be most major.*

The scene changes to the local games, archery and sack-racing, but an Olympic runner climbs the stage, the year 1996 beckons, with Pole Jump and Coxless Pairs briefly taking over for the 'golden opportunity'. These events in no way disturb the dogged and quite appalling Sir Gilbert. His wish to marry Marion despite the lack of a dowry might suggest that his motives are honourable until, to the tune of 'A frog he would a-wooing go', he boasts:

> *He's feeling frisky and frolicsome, so*
> *Tell all the girls to loosen their garters*
> *For Gilbert's methods are dirty.*

By comparison, the notorious Sheriff of Nottingham is a lesser sinner. He just wants what Lady Clare owes him, so taking a bribe from Sir Gilbert is logical, as he explains to the Chancellor's patter song from *Iolanthe*:

> *Now my motives, of course,*
> *I'll admit if I'm forced,*
> *Aren't a hundred per-cent altruistic.*
> *He has sworn to unload*
> *All the money I'm owed.*
> *Well, a fellow must be realistic.*

The Sheriff's plan is to invalidate the approaching defeat of Sir Gilbert at the hands of Marian's other suitor, that very Earl Robert of Huntingdon, in an archery contest:

SHERIFF: *Would you gain Marian?*
SIR GILBERT: *Of course I would.*
   That is, supposing always that I could.
SHERIFF: *You can.*
SIR GILBERT: *I can?*
SHERIFF: *(darkly) If 'tis, 'tis as I say.*
   And if it isn't – 'tis the other way.
SIR GILBERT: *That's lucid. But as it concerns me nearly*
   P'raps you'd just explain yourself more clearly.
SHERIFF: *The Earl of Huntingdon is sure to hit the target.*
SIR GILBERT: *Yes, I cannot shoot a bit.*
SHERIFF: *Then by the custom which is nothing new,*
   He'd marry and wed Marian.
SIR GILBERT: *That's true.*
SHERIFF: *Were he removed, you'd fill his situation.*
   You, for his riddance, without hesitation
   Must forge a Will.

SIR GILBERT: *But how, I say?*
   Where there's a will, there's always a way.
   This Will's to make you EARL. Then into prison
   We'll hurl the Earl, for making what's your'n his'n.

Earl Robert is formally dispossessed, but has too many friends at hand to be arrested; the confrontation is dramatised to a storming sextet – from *Lucia di Lammermoor*, no less. Our hero then takes off for Sherwood Forest, accompanied by the tradesmen. By the second act, his reputation as leader of an outlaw band will have spread and he is ready to challenge his enemies.

The scene is the Sheriff's apartment in Nottingham Castle. Earl Robert (alias Robin Hood) is paying a secret visit to Marian, the guest of the Sheriff's daughter, Maid Alice. He climbs in through a window.

ROBIN: *Since we last met, as outlaws have forced to roam*
   In Sherwood Forest we have made our home.
   You'll join us in the Forest?
ALICE: *Oh, we couldn't.*
MARION: *What? Go to Sherwood?*
ROBIN: *It appears sher-wouldn't.*
MARION: *How do you live?*
ROBIN: *Of taxes we are clear,*
   Everything's cheap, save venis'n, and that's deer,
   For stags are scarce. Of late we haven't seen 'em.
   My men have not got one high-deer between 'em.
MARION: *Indeed. It sounds much like running very fast to seed.*
   Twould spoil our dresses.
ROBIN: *Dress you needn't bring.*
MARION: *No dress? The bare idea of such a thing!*
ROBIN: *You'll both in archer's dress, or something near it*
   Be clad. I thought you would be 'clad' to hear it.
   You'll meet Tuck, Will – he should be here anon.
   And, Alice, you shall see my little John.
ALICE: *Your little what?*
ROBIN: *My friend, Sir John.*
ALICE: *The dear,*
   I've missed him.
ROBIN: *And he longs to have you near.*

MARION: *But this dwelling in the wood?*
    Shall we not meet the robber, Robin Hood,
    Who steals, at least so go numerous tales,
    From men, purses and from women, veils?
ALICE: *I'm told he only robs the rich and grand*
    To feed the sick and poorest in the land.
ROBIN: *I'm told he sees himself as referee*
    And in the match of life fair play to see.
    He won't hurt us.

[Will Scarlett enters]

WILL: *Captain, the coast is clear.*
    The street door's open and there's no one near.
    I have prepared the horses and the disguises
    To guard against all unforeseen surprises.
MARION: *Now for a life romantic, new and pleasant.*
ALICE: *Scenes of my childhood, ta-ta for present.*
    I've loved this place, each window, door and brick.
    And now I leave.

They celebrate with a sparkling song-and-dance act, a 'minstrel medley', based on the melodies of Stephen Foster:

MEN: *Tonight, ladies, tonight, ladies,*
    Tonight, ladies, let's haste upon our way.
    Nottingham girls, won't you come out tonight,
    Come out tonight, come out tonight?
GIRLS: *Beautiful schemers, what can we say,*
    Are you intending to lead us astray?
    Men are deceivers, so it is said,
    Never believe we are easily led.
MEN: *Way down upon the old Trent River,*
    Not far from here,
    There lies a boat that will deliver
    You from the foes that you fear.
ALL: *Hey-nonnie, ho-nonnie,*
    In the woods we'll stay,
    We'll settle there without a care
    And none shall say us nay.

Meanwhile, back in the Forest, these capers do nothing for the Merry Men who are on the point of defecting to home comforts. Tuck attempts to stir spirits with the best of Verdi:

Don't be fickle, like women as wayward as weathercocks,
Be like good Englishmen, rigid as Brighton Rocks.

Though this is the twelfth century, such prejudice will surely provoke audience reaction, but the fat Friar returns to favour with the *Flower* song from *Carmen* as a serenade to Champagne:

Thou art a nectar lovingly distilled
By Bollinger or fair Cliquot.
At each fragrant sip my heart is filled
With a euphoric and rosy glow.

Yet his taste for the drink can make him a liability, and when hero and enemy face one another, swords drawn in the gloom, he strikes the wrong man over the head, then has to retreat before the Sheriff's men. So 'Robin' is carted off to Nottingham Castle where he pretends he has gone out of his mind to put his captors off guard. The mad scene is entertaining but sadly not musical.

Marion takes over as leader of the Merry Men, fortified by *The Grand Duchess'* battle-song:

Let us ride, let us ride,
Before some cruel fate betide
That divine man of mine
Who has been ravished from my side.

Disguised as a monk wearing a cowl, which is always very impressive in opera, she requests as 'Robin's confessor' to be admitted to the Castle; this is refused, so the couple act out the *Miserere* scene from *Trovatore*. Sir Gilbert is in command, and he fires off with *Vendetta* from *Rigoletto*, but this is his last triumph.

'Robin' is eventually brought out of the Castle for execution, but Marion has had time to assemble her forces, and the madness ploy pays off; as a last favour, he is unshackled, blows his horn and Sir Gilbert is promptly ambushed. Even the Sheriff refuses to come to his aid, having developed a guilty conscience, and knowing his daughter has joined the outlaws. This is no psychological drama, so it must remain a mystery why the Sheriff is even prepared to make the ultimate sacrifice by marrying Lady Clare.

There is only one villain left and a flurry of arrows should finish him, but he has learned a Chinese trick and the arrows shoot off target, with the sheer magic at the disposal of the Players Theatre:

Alive. My juggler's trick you see has saved my jug-u- lar.

So a reprieve is granted, in gentlemanly manner, as the company prepare to celebrate several marriages promoted by this Forest romp. They must also sing the health of King Richard; this is a tradition in the story, even though he has been too busy charging around the world to attend to his royal duties. At least, he will confirm Earl Robert's inheritance.

In the intimacy of a modern 200-seat theatre, this tale has been well served with symphonic piano and fully operatic crew. Robert – 'Robin' – is the Principal Boy, and his two lieutenants the romantic tenors, all in ardent pursuit of the three young sopranos venturing into the Forest. Broad comedy comes from Lady Clare, who sometimes weighs in heavy of frame and tone. Two *buffo* roles are there to be booed, on or off pantomime horses, and Friar Tuck is a versatile baritone. Traditional airs and ten opera arias complement the entertainment.

21   *Columbus, the USA and a Pastiche*

Taking selections of a great composer's music with a specially crafted play and lyrics for an attractive pastiche was often a creative success during the 20th century, especially for very humorous stage works. During the dispute between the Greater London Council and the Government of the 1980s, satirical dialogue and lyrics were set to familiar music by Arthur Sullivan[1]:

> *My metaphors are radical, my methods are empirical,*
> *If you can spot the difference, it'll be a bloody miracle.*
> *It's hard to tell my politics apart from my cacophonies,*
> *I'm like the croaking chorus from* The Frogs *of Aristophanes.*
> *The wind of change is blowing and the ship of state has gone about,*
> *Can anyone out there please tell me what I'm on about?*

In general, using well-known music tends to prevent a new work establishing its individuality, and drawing on less familiar material of high quality is the recognised formula, especially for revealing fresh jewels by much-loved composers. The most durable pastiches, certainly in commercial terms, have been from the music of Johann Strauss II, and *Vienna Blood* is still in the repertoire of the Vienna Volksoper after almost one hundred years.

Offenbach has come in for much attention because he was so adaptable and prolific, with much excellent music hidden within failed or trifling libretti. Perhaps best known of his pastiches was *The Goldsmith of Toledo*, based mainly on his German-language operetta, *The Black Corsair*. It was performed in Germany, Vienna, Edinburgh and (1922) at Covent Garden.

Opera Rara was responsible for a new operetta undertaken with the Ulster Orchestra in 1976, the occasion being a tribute to the bi-centenary of the founding of the U.S.A. A sparkling libretto was prepared by Don White to little-known music by Offenbach for a preposterous travesty of history titled *Christopher Columbus*. When this farce reached America after Belfast and London, it was well received. The *International Herald Tribune* said it was a 'delicious piece of nonsense' and the British press lined up to offer praise; the *Daily Express* called it 'wicked, witty and entertaining'.

Some regard for reality lay in choosing as the musical framework *The Milk Carton*, an operetta written by Offenbach on his return from the U.S.A in 1876. Music was added from some twenty rarely-performed works, in particular *Vert-Vert*, *Doctor Ox* and *The Princess of Trebizond*, whose 'headache' aria becomes a 'sea-sickness' song.

Columbus, the much-travelled Italian hero, boasts of his expertise in seduction; the unfailing strategy is to propose marriage. As a result, he flees in 1488 to Spain pursued by three 'wives'. The whole lot are eventually shipped off into unchartered seas on the Queen's orders after the Grand Inquisitor has given verdict. They arrive at the island of Manhattan to set U.S. history in motion. This story of relentless action is divided neatly into four relatively short acts.

Offenbach's 'Spanish' music features in the first act, whilst the wives sing in the style of their far-off homelands. The voyage evokes serene moments, *Belle nuit* based on the Romance from *Vert-Vert*, but soon followed by 'sinking' feelings, panic, and a mutinous operatic ensemble built on the word, Columbus. In the finale, Red Indian music is fended off, but our hero displays a greed worthy of the *conquisadores* and makes a political marriage with Pocohontas. One song praises American's greatest contribution to civilisation, liquid gold known as Coca-Cola. As the anachronisms pile up, suggestions for naming the new continent: C for Columbus, I for the Queen, E for Eldorado ... quickly arrive at the anagram of 'America'; Sousa's 'Stars and Stripes forever' is heard briefly, and a benign chorale praising the New World links the finale to that once ill-fated opera, *Barkouf.*

The second act is an excellent burlesque, a unique addition to Offenbachiana with two songs in cabaret spirit. In 1879, Queen Isabella II was expelled from Spain suffering from nymphomania. Queen Isabella I had no such proclivities and was regarded as pious, not least because of her zeal in persecuting Jews and Muslims.

In this version, the sexual appetite is unkindly attributed to the first Isabella, and this condition leads indirectly to the discovery of the New World. When a fracas over bigamy occurs around Columbus near the royal palace at Seville, everyone in sight is arrested, but the Queen is intrigued to meet this great lover. Her role calls for what in a different context has been called a 'voice of brass', going outside accepted operatic requirements. To a fanfare (from *The Moon Voyage*), the Queen appears debilitated by a hang-over from the previous night's party, achieving an astounding range of notes and timbre in a confession which would raise eyebrows even if attributed to the British royal family:

A cavalry officer, simply divine, showed me his scars, or did I show him mine?
Though I know that I had a ball. I can't recall last night at all.

She hears the evidence against Columbus but dismisses the charges after he sings a passionate aria (from *The Bridge of Sighs*) praising her goddess-like beauty.

Once alone with him, she contemplates 'three days of love' but King Ferdinand returns unexpectedly, just before she has time to be caught *in flagrante delictu*, but like King Menelaus, he is easily hoodwinked. She turns a globe conveniently at hand, to explain that Columbus has been outlining an exciting scheme to find a new way 'to the East'.

Ferdinand is clearly the junior partner, as it is she who decides to make Columbus an admiral and offers to lend him the funds for the voyage at 49½% interest. As the prospect of more riches overtakes her, she refers brazenly to what she has already earned:

This jewelled halter is a souvenir of Malta,
It's made of bloodstones, greenstones, sunstones, moonstones.

[Shriek]

Don't ask me what I won it for,
Let's say I lost the battle but I won the war.

Internal rhymes and the irregular meter add much to the comic effects:

Though you may think it's
Unwise to give away my trinkets,
Tomfoolery jewellery, there's plenty more where that came from …
And I'll have them to fall back on
When the fortune that I'm sitting on is gone.

22 *A Swedish-American Comedy*

Ingmar Bergman's *Smiles of a Summer Night (1956)* is a sophisticated comedy made between a sequence of sombre films which established his international reputation. A film reflecting diverse attitudes to love and sex, where complex family relationships are revealed and subjected to change, in the Chekhov manner, not always for the better.

The problems are most acute for three males whom a weekend party places in one emotional cauldron. Fredrick Egerman is a lawyer, with some skill in squaring circles, and hopes to consummate his marriage to a child-bride, Anne, while resuming an affair with a famous actress, Desirée Armfeldt. That lady's intentions are more serious, so when visiting her after a theatre performance, he is graciously allowed to observe her removing make-up and taking a bath; but his casual attitude leads to a row instead of the bedroom.

After falling into a large puddle whilst escorting the actress home, he is caught wearing the night-shirt of her recent lover, Count Carl-Magnus Malcolm who drops by. Because his clothes are seen to be drying, Malcolm does not insist on a duel, which is fortunate, considering he is an officer of dragoon.

His wife, Charlotte, is a formidable young lady first seen taking pot-shots with a pistol as if working out a frustration. His strategy is to treat her as a confidante:

> *She had a visitor ... I turned the lawyer out, Egerman in person, still wearing my night-shirt. People have no morals nowadays ... By the way, we are invited to old Mrs Armfeldt's this weekend, along with the Egermans. If you're bored, why not visit your friend, Anne Egerman? Her husband's escapade may be news to her ... I can tolerate my wife's infidelity, but about my mistress, I'm a tiger.*

There is a story, supported by the presence of a fine old four-poster, about a king who used to stay in what is now the Armfeldt mansion and exercised *le droit de seigneur* on his prime minister's wife. Giving them separate rooms, he would press a switch which propelled her bed through a wall into his chamber. The effect is demonstrated to the Egerman's chamber-maid, Petra, by the estate's amorous steward.

'Frivolous and sensual', she has just given Egerman's son his first sexual experience, but for Henrik, a theology student, it has been an anti-climax, and humiliated, he quotes Luther on the weaknesses of the flesh. Fredrik takes the broad view, calls Petra a 'clever girl' and promises her a wage increase. He offers Henrik some advice:

> *If you are thrown, remount at once. This is a rule of love and horsemanship . . . You are confused. Lust is the plaything of youth and old men . . . A young person is always in love with himself and with love itself.*

Fredrik's presumption that older persons alone understand love infuriates his son whose distress is complete when he is slapped in the face for his carryings-on by his stepmother but with too much warmth. Anne and Henrik desire one another; she married Fredrik out of pity for a widower, but he is no more than a kind uncle, and that cannot change.

Desirée plans a weekend at her mother's country estate, in order to do 'a good turn' – or two: become Egerman's third wife, so restoring Malcolm to Charlotte, whom she promptly corners when the Malcolms arrive for the weekend:

> *Let's put our cards on the table. Your husband has a will of his own, and a libido which overwhelms him. But he's jealous over the look you gave Egerman. Men never know what is best for them, so we must help them, mustn't we? I'll make a start by fixing the seating arrangements at dinner . . .*

Their complicity grows when, observing through a window the two men playing croquet, Charlotte calls her husband a 'freebooter who turns a harmless game into a struggle for prestige'.

At dinner, Charlotte seated next to Egerman tells him she could seduce him in fifteen minutes, but the conversations across the table display more wit than sincerity. Idealistic about love, Henrik is appalled by the cynical exchanges of his elders, and rushes out expressing hatred for a father who 'responds to unhappiness with sarcasm'. Despairing through his feelings for Anne, he fails in an attempt to hang himself, falling onto the switch which propels the bed into his room, with her asleep in it. Bowing to the force of destiny, the couple elope overnight with his father's connivance.

As planned, Desirée wakes Malcolm to warn him that Charlotte and Fredrik have locked themselves into the yellow pavilion. Concerning his wife, he must also be a tiger, and confronts his rival, insisting on their being left alone to play out a game of Russian roulette. Following a pistol-shot, Malcolm emerges from the pavilion laughing:

> *I loaded them with blanks. A nobleman does not stake his life with a pen-pusher.*

Charlotte gets him back for the time being, and Fredrik, with a blackened face, is comforted by Desirée.

■ ■ ■

In her cabaret act, operatic soprano Sally Burgess asks what the American musical would now be without Stephen Sondheim. The first and second generation of distinguished composers and their collaborators have now departed, and Sondheim stands out for his special ability to fuse words and music, an eclectic who matches American idiom to classic music techniques. He was quick to appreciate the film and its musical possibilities.

Ingmar Bergman is better known for his silences than his use of music, but in this film it is applied with the lightest of touches. In the cinematic style of the late 'fifties, it is never obtrusive, but comments sensitively: ironically when during a brief truce, Desirée diverts the guests with the old German song, *Freut Euch des Lebens*, enjoy life whilst you may.

The treatment at times evokes light operas of the past, from Mozart to Lehár, and significantly, Bergman was to introduce *The Merry Widow* to a new generation of Sweden's theatre-goers. *Smiles of a Summer Night* is a period piece fixed around 1900 in a claustrophobic Swedish environment, elegant and eloquent.

Sondheim adapted the film as a tribute to the spirit of Viennese operetta, composing entirely in variants of 3–4 time. Its pervading sense of irony was to inspire some of his wittiest lyrics, with characters confronting their own anxieties, rarely communicating with others except in a conflict of minds.

Musical cross-talk, sharp changes of pace and rhythm and rich characterisation make *A Little Night Music* one of his finest scores. There are nine principal actor-singers and five others comprise an ensemble commenting on the action. In the overture, they set off like soloists warming up for an opera, then into a swirling waltz which has been referred to as Brahmsian, emulating his *Love Song Waltzes*. Yet the harmonies are much nearer to Ravel, and the musical style impressionistic, of the early decades of the twentieth century.

'The Glamorous Life' is a sarcastic patter song for two female voices, dramatising a hectic sequence of overnight stops, life controlled by worries about time and luggage, to the rhythms of a railway train.

Exciting changes of pace and a flood of images are effective in Petra's rondo, 'I shall marry the Miller's Son', where she sketches the sensual life of the poor, the affluent and royalty. From the relaxing modality of an English folk-song, she leaps into Broadway style:

> *It's a very short way from the fling that's for fun*
> *To the thigh-pressing under the table.*
> *It's a very short day till you're stuck with just one*
> *Or it has to be done on the sly.*
> *In the meanwhile, there are mouths to be kissed*
> *before mouths to be fed,*
> *And there's many a twist and there's many a bed,*
> *And a person should celebrate everything passing by.*

The Egerman family's tensions are sketched in three linked songs. *Now*, to a controlled cavalry charge, considers ways for Fredrik to seduce his own wife, and the discouraging effects of girlish chatter and household trivia. In *Later* his son, infuriated at not being treated as an adult, frets to the more sombre pitches of a cello, then goes frantically off-key. In *Soon*, Anne promises to accept the man she loves, the gloom almost disperses, and in a concluding trio, the final resolution is subtly implied.

Desirée's 13 year-old daughter, Henrika, is added to the

story as a foil; she is unsympathetic to her mother's love-life, unlike the grandmother, whose connivance is linked to her own colourful past. There are slight alterations from the original film: Fredrik and Desirée make love after the theatre visit, and the Malcolms arrive uninvited for the weekend, to the hostess's embarrassment. The croquet and moving bed sequences are omitted.

In the film, Fredrik's confiding about his marital dilemma is listened to patiently by Desirée, but Sondheim transforms this dialogue to far greater effect, with a duet, 'You must meet my wife', polite then vituperative:

FREDRIK: *She flutters.*
DESIRÉE: *How charming.*
FREDRIK: *She twitters.*
DESIRÉE: *My word.*
FREDRIK: *She floats.*
DESIRÉE: *Isn't that alarming? What is she, a bird?*
FREDRIK: *She makes me feel I'm what?*
DESIRÉE: *A very old man.*
FREDRIK: *Yes, no, but*
DESIRÉE: *No, I must meet your Gertrude.*
FREDRIK: *My Anne.*

Madam Armfeldt, once a rich and famous courtesan, is a prodigious snob, recalling in a deep voice through the mists of time her *Liaisons*, distilled passions within a leisurely existence, Mediterranean sounds and rhythms losing their urgency but not their appeal:

At the palace of the Duke of Ferrara
I acquired some position and a tiny Titian ...

The music suggests the cold, calculating world which she had known:

Liaisons? What's happened to them?
Liaisons today ... untidy.
Take my daughter. I taught her,
I tried my best to point the way.
I even called her Desirée.

'In Praise of Women' offers them scant respect, a headlong

chauvinistic anthem, with Malcolm asserting that no partner would wish to be unfaithful to him. His wife responds at a furious pace to show that they deserve each other:

The swaggering bore I'll do anything for
The air of disdain is appalling, the level of decency nil.
If he thinks that I'll always come crawling . . . I will,
I worship the ground that he kicks me around: my husband, the Pig.

In 'Every Day a Little Death', she is dragged down by male vanity, but this can turned to advantage, according to Desirée who identifies with the *femme fatale* she is playing at the theatre; the way to control a man is to gratify his self-esteem. Yet Egerman complains – if she were less perfect, he would not be in her thrall but his marriage more secure.

'A Weekend in the Country' brings the comedy into top gear, an ensemble of perpetual motion, more attractive for its irregular phrasing. Expressions of thanks are blown away by the blunt talk which precedes a pitched battle. Anne must conquer her jealousy and put on a show to depose her rival. Fredrika shows a young person's disregard for the politesse of her elders, and contempt for her mother's suitors, the negative Egerman and 'a tin soldier . . . arms, legs and brain'. Malcolm boasts of being the master tactician, and is seized with the idea of dragging his wife to the party, even on their wedding anniversary:

HE: *A weekend in the country? We should try it*
SHE: *How I wish we'd been asked.*
HE: *A weekend in the country, peace and quiet.*
SHE: *We'll go masked. Uninvited? They'd consider it odd.*
HE: *A weekend in the country, I'm delighted.*
SHE: *Oh, my God!!*
HE: *And the shooting should be pleasant if the weather's not too rough.*
     Happy birthday. It's your present,
     And you haven't been getting out nearly enough.
     A weekend in the country?
SHE: *It's perverted.*
HE: *Get my quiver and bow.*
     A weekend in the country. At exactly two-thirty we go.

To soothing clarinet tones, there is a reprise and fading out of the show's most lyrical song, 'Send in the Clowns':

DESIRÉE: *Was it a farce?*
FREDRIK: *My fault, I fear.*
DESIRÉE: *Me on a marry-go-round.*
FREDRIK: *Me as King Lear.*
How unlikely life is, to lose one's son, one's wife,
practically one's life within an hour, and yet to feel
relieved, relieved, and what's more,
considerably less ancient.

This is a time for them to balance the accounts, hoping for a coherent existence after so many years of muddle. The company play them out to a gentle Viennese waltz.

Oscar Wilde dressed as Salome

23 *Salome: Russell's Filmed Burlesque*

Why did Salome demand the head of John the Baptist?
The Biblical explanation is sketchy, that as a juvenile,
she carried out the wishes of her mother, Herodias,
who hated him.

As prisoners go, John was an embarrassment, a tiresome
fanatic. His captor, Herod Antipas, had committed so many
crimes that marrying Herodias, the wife of his own brother,
was surely not the greatest, but it was the one which John
seized upon, a form of 'incest' contrary to the laws of God.[1]

The question of Salome's motives, and why she wanted
John's head on a silver platter, interested Oscar Wilde more
than any supposed family or political intrigue. That curious
historical episode has inspired more great artists than writers,
and Wilde's play *Salome*, rests on the notion that the girl,
fascinated by John's reputation, threw herself at him, was
spurned and extracted the most gruesome revenge.

Wilde's extravagant imagery is related to the once-
fashionable 'decadent' or symbolist styles, and the
over-spiced, repetitive language which Salome addresses to
Prophet Jokanaan (John the Baptist) sounds like a parody of
The Song of Solomon:

> *It is thy mouth that I desire, Jokanaan. Thy mouth is like a band of
> scarlet on a tower of ivory. It is like a pomegranate cut with a knife
> of ivory. The red blasts of trumpets that herald that approach of
> kings, and make afraid the enemy, are not so red.*

Wilde wrote the play in French, partly to avoid the British
censor, and Sarah Bernhardt played it in London (1892), but
it remained banned in English. Dominant female heroines
were becoming a cult in European literature around the turn
of the century, and a German translation acquired notoriety
after Max Reinhardt's successful Berlin production. The play
is best known through Richard Strauss' music drama based
closely upon Wilde's text and appearing in 1905. It was the
most discussed of the year's great musical events; as one or

more critics commented, Strauss had introduced neurosis into opera. And then some.

It follows the original plot in detail, omitting a few unoperatic items, such as a debate over the existence of angels. The most dramatic scenes include the conflict of Herod with his wife, Salome's attempts to seduce the Prophet, the 'oriental' dance in which Salome gratifies Herod's request, and her lustful behaviour when presented with Jokanaan's head. This outrages even Herod who orders the guard to crush her on their pointed shields, a fate predicted by the Baptist for her mother.

The music was considered more luridly expressive than anything heard previously on a stage, matching violent emotions with harmonies and orchestration which were seemingly ultra-modern. Strauss called the work a steadily rising crescendo.

The dance has always been a special problem dramatically, though many lead sopranos are replaced for nearly ten minutes by a ballerina. She has to remove seven veils but remains wearing one garment; yet dramatically, Herod's request has no point if Salome does not complete the dance revealing herself to him bare. This was not considered an option for the first eight decades of the work's existence. Then Maria Ewing had the courage and ability to sing, dance and appear fully naked in a Covent Garden production.

Even before Wilde's play was permitted, it was used for burlesques in British music halls, despite objections about a severed head appearing. A welcome late arrival of this kind is *Salome's Last Dance*[2] (1988) by director Ken Russell, whose contribution to burlesque in the cinema has not been excelled. The film was insufficiently funded for a masterpiece, but it achieves much on a small budget.

It takes in the notorious aspects of Wilde's private life, with some predictable references, 'a handbag', and the aphorism, 'I can resist anything but temptation'. The staged performance reflects the play – and the opera – through a distorting mirror, the humour derived from a combination of literal and visual parody, and a piquant displacement of Strauss' musical effects.

In this case, Strauss is significant by his absence, the hidden agenda. Russell's empathy for his music ensures that omitting it would serve humorous purposes, such as making space for irony and innuendo. Russell seeks out contemporaneous composers, and the 'incidental' music comes from Rimsky-Korsakov, Grieg, Debussy and Satie, who are remarkably different from Strauss and from one another.

Debussy's languorous style suits the less dramatic moments at court, but his *Gigues*, a thrilling, sometimes eery orchestration of the *Keelrow*, is inserted for the scene of Salome's death. Satie's *Gymnopédies* open the film to Aubrey Beardsley's illustrations, accompany Herod's freakish wooing of Salome, and in the warm soothing tones of a 'dulcimer' bring the drama to an end. Boisterous extracts from Grieg's *Per Gynt* accompany Salome's dance and the flagellation of the Prophet.

Wilde, accompanied by his lover, Bosie, calls on Alfred Taylor whom he approvingly calls a 'brothel keeper'. Taylor, who would be sent to prison for procuring minors for Wilde, was a fairly young man then but is here presented as a disgusting old queen. He has laid on a pleasant surprise, not just another orgy.

They say that sex is the theatre of the poor. You're not going to stage The Beggars' Opera, are you?

But the date is 5 November 1892, and as Parliament had banned it, Taylor is producing a private performance, the English première of *Salome*. He asserts that, like Guy Fawkes, his friend Oscar has prepared a fuse, but a literary one, which will shake Parliament and light up the nation.

The roles are to be played by the prostitutes and their clients, acting out of admiration for Wilde's genius. The cameraman is an eccentric fellow who turns out to be Ken Russell and is on 'Ken-and-Oscar' terms with the great dramatist. He would like to make a home movie, but this is half a century too soon, so has to be satisfied with a box camera as he scampers around the room to catch the highlights of a grand drama.

He will also play a minor part, the Cappodocian, combining business with pleasure, most appropriately in this environment. Wilde hopes:

If your acting is as grossly indecent as your photographic studies, we're in for an outrageous evening.

There is some relief that Taylor is not playing Salome in

drag, and he has opted for the role of Herod. Equally at home playing his strumpet wife will be an unidentified courtesan, and Bosie has agreed to play Jokanaan, renamed John the Baptist for the film. Most problematic is likely to be the skivvy ordered to play the lead, with her quaint, below-stairs accent and, as Wilde observes, looking under-nourished. Like Strauss' version, this première will use much of the original text.

The decor is an amalgam of mock Edwardian, reminiscences of past productions of the opera, and characteristic Russell touches: faded crimson infuses the chamber, and steel grey-blue the outer vistas. The Baptist, imprisoned in a dungeon below, is raised by a serving hatch to be placed in a cage and subjected to most unsavoury treatment by ladies in modern sado-masochistic gear, with over-ripe breasts and flabby thighs. These events are enjoyed by the author, seated comfortably in the plush lounge.

Returned to the dungeon, the Prophet harangues the court with predictions about Christ and the fate of evil-doers, whilst Salome twitches with pleasure whenever he says monstrous things about her mother. He clearly revels in invective even whilst being flogged, responding to Salome's friendly advances by calling her the 'daughter' both of Babylon and of Sodom. She persists in her outrageous vamping and, as will be seen, her threat to kiss his mouth is not to be taken lightly.

This discordant dialogue, not a conversation, is accompanied by music from *Scheherezade*, magnificently sinuous and 'oriental' in contrast with Strauss' fiercely passionate declamation.

Salome thinks like a child, but is precocious in her imaginings and normally given to fleeting fancies which on this fateful day turn to a terrifying obsession. She cannot sustain a spell; spoilt brat, peeling a banana (some sixteen centuries before the Portuguese discovered it) is a provocation which excites Herod until she throws the skin onto the floor where it nearly trips him. She is years away from the seductive woman she apes, ridiculous in her crudely insinuating gestures, though when eyeing Herod she resembles a praying mantis.

Although no more than ruler of a Roman outpost, Herod the Tetrarch conforms to the Hollywood conception of a warped, pampered Emperor, repellent, obese, self-obsessed. As chief justices go, he is thoroughly unjust, attempting to deflect the Baptist's criticism by treating Herodias as the only incestuous party and accusing her of being barren.

She responds by reminding him that he killed his brother, screeching disapproval of his 'incestuous' fascination for the daughter. Her consolation is that Salome's existence enables her to throw back at him the charge of infertility.

Orthodox Jewry is represented by three midgets who request that Jesus be seized and handed over to them. Herod, as superstitious as his wife is rational, does not trouble himself with the sensational reports about Christ until hearing that he raises people from the dead. Herodias orders the Jews to be silenced, which leads to nothing worse than their being sat upon and submitted to lewd acts by three court nymphets.

The dancing highlight, such as it is, will not come from Salome, but Herod cavorting absurdly in a sea of shapely breasts and comic revellers, with the midgets once more on their feet. In an ingenious transference, the show's most exciting music is taken from Rimsky-Korsakov's opera *The Golden Cockerel*, relating to a war-mongering Russian Tsar who because of greed is destroyed.[3]

The Tetrarch offers half his kingdom in return for one dance, but Salome lounges, bored and sucking her lollipop, then capriciously agrees without stating her price. Herodias registers her disapproval by inviting two guards into an out-size trunk for strenuous exercises of which her husband seems incapable.

In static profile, Salome looks like a Hindu goddess, but her dance is a chambermaid's view of high art, even worse than a cheap night-club stripper. She throws herself around the concourse whilst Herod slobbers and giggles over her attempts at a pornographic show.

But there is real lechery afoot. The trunk rattles loudly, Wilde who has been comforting Herod's gold-adorned page takes him behind a curtain, and even the Baptist crawls up for a peep. Primitive rituals are evoked in an accelerating symphonic movement, but Grieg's music never suggests sensuality.[4]

When Salome disrobes, the hallucinating ruler imagines her in double, then as a hermaphrodite. After the dance, her

performance can only improve; her finest moment is enjoying Herod's abasement, mischievously articulating her
demand for John the Baptist's head. The mother interrupts
her sexual pleasures to express loud approval.

Herod accedes, but cringes with fear as 'the holy man' is
executed off-stage by a huge Nubian carrying a terrifying
sword. Finally, the Prophet's stoicism denies Salome the
pleasure of hearing him suffer.

In the following scene, she acts out luridly sadistic feelings
for the man who has callously rejected her love and whose
head can now be rested on a plinth, then in her hands, finally
to be kissed. This is to the accompaniment of gentle, passionless music by Debussy and Satie. Herod is outraged, ordering
her death at the end of a spear.

Wilde has been growing bored with his creation, but Thes-
pian enthusiasm must be displayed, and in a gratuitous insult,
he likens the show to *verismo*, current Italian realism.[5] The
female who has played Herodias and claims to perform
regularly as Lady Macbeth before royalty takes centre-stage in
the absence of any other real women. Wilde congratulates
her, as the equal of Sarah Bernhardt, except that she lacks a
wooden leg. When a policeman out of *The Pirates of Penzance*
calls, she responds with a 'Tarantara', to which the dramatist
objects: 'Not *The Pirates*, I'd hate to share a double-bill with
Gilbert and Sullivan'; but he'd like a replay, with himself as
the Prophet and Bosie as Salome.

Wilde would be photographed later playing the role of
Salome, but the evening's pleasures end abruptly. Three
years in advance of reality, he is arrested for 'gross sexual
indecency' and 'corruption of minors', along with Taylor for
'running a disorderly house'. The policeman has put the
'actress' down as an 'ore', but she does not want to travel in a
horse-box with two common criminals, and gives her name as
Lady Alice Fitz-Kensington Windsor – presumably a royal
bastard? On the question of the alleged murder of a chamber-
maid, she has the last words:

> *Murdered? Nonsense, it was just death by misadventure. She
> slipped on a banana skin.*

24 'Cabaret': A Berlin Story

Cabaret, one of the best American musicals of the past 50 years, is conceptually very different from *The Three-penny Opera*, but was influenced by it and the two works share interesting points of reference. Sharp ironic contrast runs through each, the disparity between the musical ambience and the realities of life intensifying the black humour.

It was fired by Berlin's lighter entertainment scene of the late 1920s, the music, fashions and the clubs, their ambience and styles of dancing. The lyrics of Fred Ebb were added to an adaptation of John Van Druten's play *I am a Camera*, based on the part-autobiographical Berlin novels of Christopher Isherwood. John Kander's music is impressively inspired by the period.

Cabaret artiste, Sally Bowles, is feckless, and scarcely has her feet on the ground even when not dancing. Three of her up-beat songs make statements about herself: 'Perfectly marvellous', 'Life is a Cabaret', and 'Don't tell Mama'. If her stage talent does not guarantee her job security, a liaison with the Club manager helps, but emotional shallowness spells persistent failure for her personal relations.

During a dance routine, she first sees a young American writer, Cliff Bradshaw, then contacts him by singing a telephone song; certain Berlin dance-halls had 'phones placed on tables as an encouragement to flirting. They enjoy a cool friendship until, unable to fend adequately for herself, she moves in with him; soon she can only guess who is the father when she falls pregnant.

The Kit-Kat Club, with its sleazy owners and hostesses, presents a leg-show, thigh-thrusting and exaggerated vulgarity, fired off by a quirky *Conferencier* (master of ceremonies) who keeps the clients laughing with teasing innuendo and a line in outrageous hype. He refreshes jaded spirits with the cosmopolitan gloss of the solo 'Willkommen, Bienvenus, Welcome'. John Kander matches the very incisive lyrics with originality and wit in composing for comic scenes, such as a 'three in a bed' nonsense song, and a 'multi-national' caberet of mature dancing girls.

The show has two shock routines. One is an anthem of solidarity which shows Nazi ideology penetrating these low levels; the other has the Host dancing with a gorilla to the words, 'If you could see her as I do'. This variant on the notion that beauty exists only in the mind lights up a genuine non-racist parable, and comments neatly on the sub-plot. This concerns a middle-aged couple deprived of a life together by what will soon become Nazi racial laws; one a Jew, the other Cliff's landlady.

That role, often resigned or bitter, could have been written for chanteuse Lotte Lenya, Kurt Weill's widow and since Berlin days, the authentic interpreter of his songs. With her inimitable style of husky sung-speech, she was the first actress to play the part.

On his first train journey to Berlin, Cliff is befriended by Ernst who is smuggling goods into Germany. He is not offended until Ernst threatens the 'Aryan' landlady that her business will suffer if she marries the Jew. He calculates the financial advantages of being a Nazi, typical of millions who would profit a few years later from the corruption and black market prevalent in German-occupied Europe.

A Nazi propaganda sheet around 1930 described Berlin as 'a melting-pot of everything evil ... prostitutes, drinking houses, Marxism, Jews, strippers, negroes dancing, and all the vile options of modern art'. Yet the Club was not politically 'subversive', and the sleaze was of no concern to the Nazis, so it would not be closed down; only the communists would have gone so far. Sally is morally pragmatic, although she cannot even assess her narrow self-interest. She and most of the entertainers would not concern themselves with the sinister political developments.

The action covers several years, and for some time, Cliff like most people treats the Nazis as a joke. He finally comes to blows with Ernst, and as a result, is beaten up by Party comrades at the Club. Its final scene points to the arrival of the new political masters; the songs do not need much revising, but the music takes on even more strident tones, and the dancing continues imitating the goose-step, but no longer in ridicule. There are token Nazi symbols, and the Host just adds a swastika to his armband.

English-born Sally has no sense of the coming danger, even as a British passport holder, and no intention of quitting the Club, even though Cliff is determined to leave Germany. Their story ends with his anger over her abortion, the ultimatum that she should accompany him and his departure alone.

In 1972 a much revised version of *Cabaret* appeared as a film, directed by Bob Fosse, and its achievements were regarded by the critics even more favourably; such a successful adaptation of a quality musical was a rare event for the film industry, thanks greatly to an improved musical score, Fosse's inventiveness and previous experience as a stage producer.

The sub-plot of the elderly couple and their sad songs was removed, so that the cabaret includes nearly all of the musical score. The role of Sally Bowles, now an American, becomes more central, Liza Minnelli's riveting performance on-stage reaching the heights with two spectacular additions.

An eccentric duet sung at double speed and in unison by Sally and the Host sets off the most dynamic of all the dance routines and blows away illusions to the words 'Money makes the World go round'. It is the crudest of ripostes to the humanistic spirit in music, and the belief that love makes the world go round, a theme in Mozart's *Magic Flute* and several musicals.

Songs which put a cheerful gloss on farewells may have a rare appeal, and the film introduces a compelling one for Sally, backed by an acrobatic chorus. It has a rhythmic verve often associated with Jewish or Eastern European styles, and the excitement of acceleration which nearly all commercial songs in our times seem to deny themselves. There is a clear affinity with Edith Piaf's 'Those were the days':

> *Bye-bye, mein lieber Herr, Auf Wiedersehen mein Herr,*
> *It was a fine affair but now it's over*
> *And though I used to care, I need the open air.*
> *You're better off without me, mein Herr.*

Minnelli is first seen in heavy make-up looking like a clown; her eyes reflect the humour of the situations which tend to arise whenever she is in unfamiliar company. Cliff, now an

Englishman, Brian, is fond of and protective towards Sally; she is a 'natural' who could effortlessly break the ice at a party, but soon overstay her welcome.

Interrupting a formal English conversation class, she creates less embarrassment than bewilderment, then hilarity. Yet the comic veneer detracts from her sexual appeal and her self-image as a *femme fatale* is preposterous, as Brian shouts in exasperation.

Joel Grey, previously admired as the Club's Host, repeats the role in the film, establishing the definitive interpretation, a goblin entertainer, virtuoso of comic mime, patter and the walking-stick, sometimes an accomplished chorus girl.

Their timing, with transvestites adding a grotesque touch, is now perfected to the syncopation and brassy instruments of a jazz band, in which they put on a show of virtuosity. Using a cramped stage in close-up gives the dancing sequences a more precipitous impact, but the professionalism now belongs to a very superior night-club.

Brian shares Sally with Max, who reflects the attitude of many affluent Germans. They regarded Hitler as an upstart, lacking the intelligence or know-how, so 'controllable' in the long run: rather the Nazis than the 'Reds'.

Mindless Nazi propaganda about 'a well-organised international conspiracy of Jewish bankers and communists' is repeated in Brian's lodgings, and he responds with dismissive English humour. Yet later, when very distressed, he acts out of character with aggressive intent towards two storm-troopers and ends up needing hospital treatment.

He is obliged to give language lessons, where two young adults meet, fatefully in the ironic sub-plot. One has come to live in Berlin because it is a tolerant city, and can offer anonymity which would conceal his Jewish origins. He even has notions about playing the gigolo, but is about to grow up emotionally. He becomes deeply challenged through falling in love with the second student, a beautiful Jewess. At this point, the Nazis are not yet in power, so their brutal victimisation of her family is illicit, carried out by street thugs.

Unwilling to lose her, he admits to being Jewish and receives her family's approval for their marriage, with consequences to be guessed at.

Beyond the play, the film shows something of life in Berlin

away from the Club and the lodgings, with the cabaret used imaginatively as an ironic commentary on the action throughout, the music often synchronised to dramatic events.

Compared with the stage version, the film intensifies the impact of the song directed at youthful hopes, 'Tomorrow belongs to me', composed in classic German folk style and resembling the melody of *Die Lorelei*, but heroic in expression. It shows a positive feature of nationalism, the propagation of German culture through politics.

Evil looms seductively and the Devil has many good tunes. This one is conspicuously beautiful, reaching through to the soul, like the finest of popular classics. In a sunny Biergarten, a youth sings the words ingratiatingly, the focus at first directed onto his handsome features. As the melody increases in urgency, the camera range extends to reveal a swastika on his raised arm, and his manner becomes more arrogant; the warm sense of fellowship induces his audience to rise, join in singing and give the Nazi salute. Observed generations later, their gullibility in face of the disease of Nazism makes for intense dramatic irony. One old man, uncomprehending, remains seated, a shadow from the past, though he might once have marched to war with such songs.

Brian asks the impassive Max:

Do you still think you can control them?

Appendix:
Ken Hill and the Phantoms at the Opera

British producer and writer, Ken Hill, has made a unique contribution to the cause of musical comedy and pastiche in our times, and was in the best sense a populariser. His achievements are also recognised abroad, with stage successes on the Continent and in the USA.

It was during preparations for *Zorro – The Musical* at the Theatre Royal, Stratford East, that Mr Hill tragically died in 1995. A fund has now been established to encourage staged enterprises such as associated him with that innovative London theatre and the Newcastle Playhouse.

Zorro was based on a one-time kids' matinée hero, suitably 'over the top'; with the use of lively songs from Spanish *zarzuelas*, an amusing adventure-musical was achieved, a fitting tribute to Mr Hill. It had followed at Stratford soon after *Bel Ami*, an adaptation of Maupassant's cynical novel, an attractive period piece given atmosphere by Offenbach's music.

Ken Hill also succeeded with themes which touched on the impossible, applying a degree of sensibility which avoided bathos: the excitement and humour were to come from genuine tension, as he wrote in stage directions. Neat allusions would add a lighter touch; for example, in *The Invisible Man* (1993), he adapted 1886's chauvinist song from the music halls, 'By Jingo', to 1904, the Kaiser and the *Entente Cordiale*.

He enlivened the old tale of *The Phantom of the Opera* with witty dialogue. Mephisto's breath-taking entry is sabotaged when his neck gets tangled in a curtain rope, but he survives to argue philosophically with the Phantom as to which of them really exists. An interesting word is invented: *chandelierised*, to be crushed by a huge chandelier dropped from a great height. In this way, the villainess, soprano Carlotta, is eliminated from the script, but the Phantom stays till the end before killing himself.

The work is an accomplished pastiche, the musical era faithfully reflected in 18 opera arias, from Gounod, Offenbach and Verdi, with single items from seven other outstanding 19th century composers, comprising the entire musical score.

* * *

The Phantom of the Opera (1915) was an inferior novel lacking even psychological interest, a relic from the previous century's style of melodrama. It would probably have disappeared without trace except that Hollywood thought it suitable material for a silent film. Some twenty years later, it was made into perhaps the most eccentric film to emerge from Hollywood during World War II, with the plot changed to heighten the sadistic effects. In those days, genuine opera was thought intolerable for American films, so a tasteless concoction was made from a vocal adaptation of Tchaikovsky's Fourth Symphony. A recent American film has the Phantom usurping, from a theatre box, the title role in Gounod's *Faust*. There is some humour in a sub-plot, but the sentimentality is overloaded by the invention of the Phantom's father and mother.

This story is at best suited for burlesque, which is not lacking in Andrew Lloyd-Webber's London version, though the enthusiastic audiences are scarcely prepared for it. Most curious for our account is the opening scene, the selling of memorabilia from a very old operatic production. These relate to *Robert le Diable*, once mentioned with hushed breath, but here no more than grist to an auctioneer's mill. Yet inexplicably, none of Meyerbeer's splendid music is to be heard. Surely the choice of opera was not random? Perhaps it was included with a special sense of occasion; on this same theatre site (a fire intervening), the opera had been performed in 1847, and with Jenny Lind making her London début.

Notes

2. Paris-London: The Versatile Monsieur Hervé

1. The term opera *bouffe* is derived from the Italian, opera *buffa*, musical entertainment based on comic characters and situations (see also page 82), a more sophisticated development from the 1850s. *Les bouffes* would refer to comic actors or clowns.
2. A 'classical' operetta, admired by such formidable critics as Clément and de Banville; there is a famous poster by Chéret.
3. Illustrated on this book's back cover.

4. Tales of Offenbach

1. Luther's *Ein' feste Burg* (A firm Stronghold) was adapted for a J.S. Bach cantata. It is the leading motif in *The Huguenots*, where it is built up into the powerful orchestral Prelude. A typical Offenbach irreverence, recognised as a good joke in the 1850s, especially as Luther's hymn was being used increasingly in solemn compositions, e.g. in Mendelssohn's *Reformation* Symphony.
2. Rossini composed many light songs (see page 88), including the *Cat duet*. Saint-Saens' *Carnival of Animals* and Prokofief's *Peter and the Wolf* are popular concert suites.
3. 'Twinkle, twinkle, little Star', known by many titles in Europe, the melody also used by Haydn and Dohnanyi.
4. Literary plots often centred on questions of family association, status and property rights, from classical Greek drama through to Victorian novels, and many opera climaxes. They were an obvious target for ridicule.
5. A *rataplan* imitates a drum-beat, a march rhythm often used in opera as a call to arms, notably in Meyerbeer and Verdi.
6. The Underworld is ruled by Pluto (a Roman god), or Hades (Greek). Cerberus is the guardian-dog which pre-

vents souls from escaping across the Rivers Lethe or Styx. Those waters bring oblivion of the past (hence our word, *lethal*), which explains why Pluto's servant, John Styx, is so forgetful, with his tiresome bumbling around Eurydice. The three judges who allot souls to their final residences also appear in the 1874 version, in order to bring Pluto to heel.

7. Jupiter's metamorphoses in the cause of seduction feature often in literature and art, also in R. Strauss' opera, *The Loves of Danae*.

8. The London première (October 1875) lasted until nearly midnight before the audience emerged from the Philharmonic hall into darkest Islington, where, it would seem, there was a shortage of elephants. The audience were delayed by a flurry of puns which had been cunningly placed in the translation. The chance to escape from a high prison was called a 'rope-ortunity'.

9. Court scenes were central to Verdi's *Don Carlos,* written for Paris in 1867, so the allusion was topical.

10. In Bad Ems, Offenbach performed his new works in German for the Prussian court every summer during the 1860s. He also took the waters for his arthritis, gambled and enjoyed extra-marital pleasures.

11. It featured the renowned '30s operetta singer, Yvonne Printemps.

12. Well-produced spectaculars in New York or London are immensely costly, so impresarios aim at a mass market, not too discriminating, and impressed by heavy advance publicity. The fashion is nostalgic, conducive to imitation rather than parody.

13. *Lurette* (1880) was orchestrated by Delibes, the first version in English being performed three years later. The melody of 'The Blue Danube' became a duet, 'In London Town', and the *Era* commented that Offenbach must have hoped to kill it off by ridicule. However, the audience enjoyed it greatly, along with an interpolated Hervé song.

Mlle Moucheron (1880) is a girls' boarding school romp. For the 1980 Offenbach Centenary, BBC Radio prepared a fizzing version set in Scotland, with a 'Miss Jean Brodie' sound-alike as teacher.

8. Sullivan and Parody

1. Coloratura singing is unique, immensely exciting to audiences. Verdi and Gounod were among the last of the best-known composers to write for it, and the latter's *Romeo and Juliet* (1867) could have been the model.
2. See Chapter 4, note 5.
3. The witch, Azucena, narrates how in a gesture of revenge she threw a baby into the fire, later discovering it was her own (*Di quella pira*).
4. Following Wagner, chromaticism was used very emotively by young composers from the 1880s, and in the late religious works of Gounod which could fill massive halls, such as the Crystal Palace.

9. Berlin Follies

1. Künnecke wrote also several works in English for New York and London, using texts drawn from Dickens, Kipling and the Nelson-Emma Hamilton story.
2. In the 1990s, the author saw it in two cities. In Berlin, with Ute Lempe, it failed through production problems, and in London it was scarcely a commercial success, though the critics liked it. The London Lola, talented young Kelly Hunter, stated publicly that London audiences were not prepared to face a challenge. About six other musicals closed quickly at the time.

10. Black Humour: The Threepenny Opera

1. Town criers and street singers used to oblige with details of crimes, etc. The *Morität* was in such a Berlin tradition.
2. The song became a popular 'hit' much later outside Germany: from Künnecke's *Cousin from Nowhere.*
3. This is apparent in the communistic film version which however Brecht did not acknowledge. Made by G.W. Pabst in German and French just after the end of the 'silent' period, it was rather static, and the musical impact is disappointing, though a film of historical interest.

11. Rossini and Opera Buffa

1. The selection of composers is recent, used in a Viennese revival but not at the London Guildhall production of 1987. That choice would not have been made in 1825 when Mozart was under-valued and J.S. Bach scarcely known, though there was nothing he did not know about rhythm.

2. *A capella* writing is a device which Rossini had often used to most compelling effect, in tragedy or comedy; after dramatic changes of fortune, hesitant or repetitively, the characters on stage confide their apprehensions or bewilderment to steadily rising tension. The court's reaction to Duncan's murder in Verdi's *Macbeth* is a magnificent example.

3. The ruling Russian aristocracy in those days would have held native Russian music in contempt, favouring French and Italian styles. Much later, Mussorgsky and other nationalists began to research and use folk music.

12. An Italian Falstaff

1. Puccini took ideas and sometimes plots from operas recently composed by others: e.g. *Manon Lescaut, La Bohème, Madame Butterfly*.

2. This episode is an inspired addition from *Henry IV*.

13. An English Falstaff

1. Elgar was planning a comic opera just before his death and fragments have been recorded. Vaughan Williams wrote an extravaganza, *The Poisoned Kiss*, using the rhythms of the 1920s.

2. With his strong sense of history, Vaughan Williams has written unfavourably of the effects of courtly music introduced by the Normans, at the expense of the more important English folk styles.

3. This is the second melody in the popular *Fantasia on Greensleeves*.

4. The distinguished folk-song, 'Peg o'Ramsey'.

5. The timing is as in Shakespeare. Verdi altered it to 'from 2 till 3' as musically more suited to the Italian text.

14. Humour in Richard Strauss

1. If so, it was a compliment, Richard being one of the 20th century's greatest melodists. The mood of the two waltzes is markedly different, Josef's wistful, the other exultant.
2. The full correspondence of these two men is easily available through public libraries.

17. A Hungarian Fantasy

1. Hungary's right-wing governments contributed to the farce by retaining the title 'Kingdom' from 1919 to 1944, even though there was no King. Then they went to their doom as Hitler's allies.
2. Gipsy bands were very popular in Western Europe as recently as the 1960s, from Piccadilly's 'White Bear' to Berlin's 'Zigeunerkeller'. At the Richmond Castle (alongside the Thames), the band was replaced one day by a juke-box – louder and cheaper.
3. Imitations of farmyard animals are common in folk music. There is such a song in Kodaly's folk-opera, *The Spinning Room*, and an American one arranged by Aaron Copland.
4. The Ruthenians are Slavs, closest to the Ukrainians with whom they are now joined. Hungarians are remote linguistically from everyone else.
5. Moving vocal passages, such as the patriotic duet, 'This Side of the Tisza, beyond the Danube', are transferred to a larger cimbalon producing warm, dulcimer-like sounds. When the Suite first appeared, it gave many Westerners a first hearing of an instrument which, in a smaller version, remains prominent with clarinet, violin and double-bass in traditional folk quartets – and larger combinations.

18. A Wagner Parody

1. Beckmesser was a bad critic but a worse singer. He attempted to steal a song prepared for the Mastersingers' competition, but landed a spoof version, and sang it, only to earn the ridicule of the whole town.

19. Shostakovitch in Lighter Mood

1. The confidence of these three interlopers places them as NEP-men, with a financial interest in the work-place resulting from the New Economic Policy of the mid-1920s which permitted a partial return to capitalism. Stalin's rule soon ended this.
2. It includes the lyrical slow movement of the Second Piano Concerto, which looks back to the nineteenth century.
3. Now widely known as the third movement of the misleadingly titled *Jazz Suite number 1*.
4. Russian for the higher ranks of the Communist Party.
5. This is followed by a fanfare taken from *Rayok*, a satirical cabaret piece, 'subversive' and therefore never performed publicly. There is little reference to *Rayok* in standard books, so MacBurney's research is of special interest, indicating that more music was transferred from *Rayok* to *Cheryomushki*.
6. In the film, Baburov is not a clown, so his eccentricity has been played up to amusing effect by Pimlico Opera. In Russian tradition, 'wisdom' or criticism was often put into the mouth of a buffoon or village idiot, a *yurodivy*. There is a 'holy fool' in *Boris Godunov*.

21. Columbus, the USA and a Pastiche

1. New lyrics to the Major General's patter song (from *The Pirates of Penzance*), taken from *The Metropolitan Mikado* (1985) by Ned Sherrin and Alistair Beaton.

23. Salome: Russell's Filmed Burlesque

1. It was an offence under English law even in the nineteenth century, though W.S. Gilbert ridiculed that situation in *Iolanthe*.
2. Veston Pictures, 1988, with Imogen Millais Scott (as Salome), Glenda Jackson (Herodias), Stratford Johns (Herod) and Nickolas Grace (Wilde).
3. It is remarkable that *The Golden Cockerel* (1909) passed the Tsar's censors, presumably because it was 'only' opera. It would be perfect for film treatment by Russell, ironic and enigmatic throughout. The Tsar has to surrender his ill-

gotten gains, whilst the illusory love of a beautiful, exotic queen is the instrument of his downfall. The extract relates to the Tsar's exultation, hubris and death at the hands of a manipulating wizard.

4. 'In the Hall of the Mountain King' from *Per Gynt*. Grieg was shocked when first hearing the sensuality of Delius' music and urged restraint on his younger friend.

5. Another *in-joke*. *Verismo* plays were doom-laden and ended with disaster, but the music could be immensely moving. The genre was very fashionable in the years between late Verdi and Strauss' *Salome*. Puccini, Giordano and others gave them beauty and great popularity, e.g. *La Bohème*, *Fedora*.

Index of Names in the Chapters

Recent JUVENTUS paperback publications available through all booksellers:

New Chekhovs

NEW CHEKHOVS
ISBN 0 9524964 4 5

Important additions to what we may know of Chekhov's writings in translation, including two plays first produced in London in 1997 by Elizabeth Gamberoni who has recently translated all three of these.

The longest play, in 7 scenes, is a dramatization of one of Chekhov's excellent short stories. These are given due credit in a poignant introduction about his life and works.

The other play appearing for the first time in English is a short comedy revealing the appalling state of dental surgery in the Russia of the 1880s, with Chekhov writing as a medical man and smiling through misfortunes.

ROMATICISM & MELODY
(Essays for Music-Lovers by
George Colerick)
246 Pages
ISBN 0 9524964 2 9

A celebration of a superlative era of melody-making, from the 1820s to the 1950s, from Beethoven to Bernstein. The topics range from the early Brahms of the Piano Quartets to the use of Romantic music in Ken Russell's films, the young Bernard Shaw as music critic and Wagnerite, aspects of 20th century British music, Viennese and Parisian music theatre, Transylvanian folk-culture and of Soviet music policy within the Russian tradition. Over one half of the 26 chapters relate to the 20th century.

This book is 'in cumulative effect refreshing in its directness and enthusiasm ... full of comic and curious lore'. (BBC Music Magazine, November 1995)

In the first two years, it has taken its place in hundreds of libraries – public, music and school.